Managing the *New* One-Person Library

KU-267-354

GRIFFITH COLLEGE DUBLIN
SOUTH CIRCULAR ROAD DUBLIN 8
TEL: (01) 4150490 FAX: (01) 4549209
email: library@gcd.ie

025.1
STC

Managing the
New One-Person Library

Guy St Clair
Joan Williamson

BOWKER
SAUR ●

London • Melbourne • Munich • New York

© 1992 Bowker-Saur, a division of Reed Elsevier (UK) Ltd

All rights reserved. No part of this publication may be reproduced or transmitted in any form or by any means (including photocopying and recording) without the written permission of the copyright holder except in accordance with the provisions of the Copyright, Designs and Patents Act 1988 or under the terms of a licence issued by the Copyright Licensing Agency, 90 Tottenham Court Road, London W1P 9HE. The written permission of the copyright holder must also be obtained before any part of this publication is stored in a retrieval system of any nature. Applications for the copyright holder's written permission to reproduce, transmit or store in a retrieval system any part of this publication should be addressed to the publisher.

Warning: The doing of any unauthorized act in relation to a copyright work may result in both a civil claim for damages and criminal prosecution.

British Library Cataloguing in Publication Data
A catalogue record for this title is available from the British Library

Library of Congress Cataloging-in-Publication Data
A catalog record for this book is available from the Library of Congress

First edition *Managing the One-Person Library* 1986
Second edition *Managing the New One-Person Library* 1992
Reprinted 1995

Published by Bowker-Saur, Maypole House, Maypole Road,
East Grinstead, West Sussex RH19 1HU, UK
Tel: +44(0)1342 330100 Fax: +44(0)1342 330191
E-mail: lis@bowker-saur.co.uk
Internet Web site: http://www.bowker-saur.co.uk/service/

Bowker-Saur is part of REED REFERENCE PUBLISHING

ISBN 0-86291-630-5

658

Typesetting by Typographics, Whitstable, Kent
Printed on acid-free paper
Printed and bound in Great Britain by Antony Rowe Ltd, Chippenham, Wiltshire

Foreword

Dr David R. Bender
Executive Director, Special Libraries Association

I am delighted and honoured to have been asked to write about *Managing the New One-Person Library*. As Guy St Clair and Joan Williamson state in the book, it was through the interest and encouragement of the members of the Special Libraries Association that they were encouraged to bring to fruition their ideas about one-person librarianship and its validity as a subject for study. Today SLA, with an international membership approaching 15 000, stands in the forefront of research and professional support for the one-person and one-professional library community, with a large number of the Association's members working in one-person or one-professional libraries and information centres. The dramatic growth of interest in the subject within the organization, culminating in the Solo Librarians Caucus growing in less than two years into a fully-fledged division – now with 440 members – attests to the fact that one-person and one-professional librarianship is here to stay.

When *Managing the One-Person Library*, the earlier edition of this book, was published in 1986, it was hailed not only as comprehensive, educational and informative, but also as indispensable. For the first time, a one-person librarian could turn to one source for everything from the nuts and bolts of management to the latest in library thinking about library automation, particularly as it applied to the one-person library. Now, with *Managing the New One Person Library*, St Clair and Williamson have come full circle. In addition to providing the basics of library and information services management for those who work alone or with minimal assistance, they also provide, for the modern one-person librarian, tips for daily success in the library, the latest – and most innovative – ideas about advocacy for the library and practical and valuable instruction about marketing the library.

Additionally, and as important as anything else in the book, St Clair and Williamson offer their opinions about the value of one-person libraries to the organizations they serve. Their vision of how good, solid management practices affect the success of the one-person library or information centre will be an invaluable resource for the readers of this book, and much of what they say on this subject can be transferred – and is equally appropriate – to the library and information services profession at large.

The special libraries community is proud of this work in one-person librarianship. In 1989, Guy St Clair's efforts were recognized by the Special Libraries Association when he was given SLA's most prestigious award, the SLA Professional Award. Having been given only thirty times in the association's 82-year history, the award was an appropriate honour to bestow on St Clair. The citation read: 'Guy St Clair is credited in the information profession with recognizing the role of one-person libraries in the library community. He is also known as an author, lecturer and consultant.' In 1990, St. Clair was elected President of SLA, a position he holds until June 1992, as he continues to serve the profession – and the specific branch of the profession – that obviously means much to him.

Joan Williamson, too, has been and continues to be a valuable member of the special libraries community. As a speaker and author on a variety of topics dealing with the management of the small library, particularly the training and education of the one-person/one-professional library manager, Williamson is recognized in the United Kingdom for her expertise. In the Special Libraries Association, she plays an important role as the single international member of SLA's Networking Committee and as the Bulletin Editor for the European Chapter.

As I wrote in 1986 in the Foreword to the precursor of this book (and I am happy to repeat here): I congratulate Guy St Clair and Joan Williamson on writing this book. It will long be the source of assistance to those working in one-person/one-professional libraries.

Contents

Chapter One

Introduction

In the six years since *Managing The One–Person Library* was published, developments in the field of one–person librarianship have progressed remarkably. The publication of the book in 1986 called attention to a unique area of library management for which most educators and practitioners had little prior knowledge. There was, to be sure, the American monthly, *The One–Person Library: A Newsletter for Librarians and Management*, which had been in publication for a couple of years, and Aslib's One–Man Band Group was holding regular meetings to bring British one–person librarians together, and this group, too, produced a newsletter. In the library profession at large, however, scant attention was paid to those librarians who worked alone, and when the subject was raised, the general reaction was usually one of mild uninterest or a shrug of the shoulders. One–person librarianship, as a subset of the library and information services profession, meant little.

All that has changed now. Today, each of the four branches of library and information services (that is, librarianship and information management as practised in public, academic, school and special libraries) gives attention to the management of the one–person library. Special librarianship in particular has taken a leading role in addressing the needs of the single–staff practitioner, obviously because so many special libraries are managed by one person. Continuing education courses addressing the special requirements of one–person librarianship continue to proliferate. After a few years of indecision about whether one-person librarianship should be accepted as a proper subset of library and information services, graduate programmes in library and information studies are now bringing one–person librarianship into their special libraries courses, and similar attention will likely be given in general management programmes at some future date, as more public, academic, and school training programmes recognize that many of their practitioners will be employed in single-staff situations.

There have been other developments as well. In 1986, Aslib's nascent One–Man Band Group was the only organized body giving attention to the needs of the single–staff librarian. Today the Solo Librarians Division of the Special Libraries Association and a variety of other formal and informal support groups are actively bringing professional management techniques - and networking opportunities - to those who work in one–person libraries. The programmes and services which these groups offer are today the primary vehicle through which one-person librarians can enhance and develop their professional expertise. In doing so, these library managers thus position themselves in their organizations and communities as library and information professionals to be reckoned with. They are taken seriously.

Defining the one–person library

In the first edition of this book, we described the one–person library as one in which all of the work is done by the librarian. In some libraries this work is limited to professional duties, with support staff to handle clerical routines and other tasks in the library (sometimes called the 'one–professional' library). In other libraries and information units, the librarian literally does *all* the work, from readers' services to emptying the waste–paper baskets. Between these two extremes are many people, some trained, some not, who have the title 'librarian' and who perform duties related to the library in the community or the parent organization in which they are employed (or for which they serve as volunteers, for many one–person librarians, working in such institutions as small museums, churches, historical societies, charitable organizations etc., do not receive remuneration for the work they do).

These one–person librarians are found in all types of library work. Some people are surprised to learn, for example, that one–person libraries can be found in academic institutions, yet many are there. Even in very large universities, departmental libraries serving specific faculties are often managed by one librarian, with additional help, during term-time, sometimes provided by student assistants. Public libraries, of course, constitute a large segment of one–person librarianship, for not only are there literally thousands of rural libraries in the United States run by one employee, but many other public libraries have branch libraries employing one person who is in charge of all library services for that branch. School libraries, too, are frequently administered by one library or media specialist, who must tackle the same kind of problems and service requirements as the single–staff practitioner in public and academic settings.

It is in special libraries that the single librarian has remained the standard, and today the library operated as a one–person unit is still most often found in a non–public situation. In the United Kingdom and the United States, one–person libraries and information centres exist in such varied organizations as legal, accounting and computing firms, learned societies, agricultural institutes, engineering and chemical companies, research institutions, private clubs, trade associations, hospitals and schools, food and drink companies, cathedrals, marketing organizations, as small offshoots of larger governmental libraries, and in just about any other company or organization which has need of library or information services.

Our original definition from 1986 continues to be valid, but attention to the subject of one–person librarianship in the last few years has brought about several refinements, some of interest, some merely different ways of saying the same thing (the 'single–staff' librarian, for example, or the 'minimal–staff' library). Perhaps the most useful definition – and one we wish we had thought of in 1986 – is used in the Special Libraries Association (SLA), an international organization of some 13 000 members. Special librarians define themselves as library and information professionals who provide focused, working information to a specialized clientele on an ongoing basis, to further the mission and goals of a particular parent company or organization, and they often use the terms 'special librarians' and 'information professionals' interchangeably.

In 1988, in order to provide a forum for networking activities and a mechanism through which librarians who work alone could benefit from programmes, educational workshops and the like, a group of one–person librarians in the SLA organized themselves into a caucus within the organization. The group, led by Martha Rose Rhine of the Olin Corporation in Marion, Illinois, chose the name 'solo librarians' because, as they said, OPL Resources, Ltd., the publishers of *The One–Person Library* newsletter, was already using the term in a commercial application and the group wished to avoid confusion. In addition, as Rhine noted at the time, 'the word solo has the image of featured artists with talents exceeding those of the accompanying group'.

As they struggled to define their potential members, the organizers of SLA's Solo Librarians Caucus realized that much of what is said about one–person library management is equally applicable to one–professional librarianship. Despite having some minimal assistance, these librarians and information professionals also found themselves benefiting from the new interest in one–person librarianship as a subset of library and information management. The library manager belonging to this group is, of course, the 'professional' working in a library or information setting, although (further complicating matters) 'professional' in this case refers primarily to managerial responsibility. The term does not necessarily relate to graduate training in library and information science, for such graduate training is assumed, at least in theory.

Reasoning that their new group would be of interest and value to both one–person and one–professional librarians, the organizers of the Solo Librarians Caucus chose to describe themselves with a definition that would include both, and theirs is the best definition we have found: 'the isolated librarian or information collector/provider who has no professional peers within the immediate organization'. Using this definition, the solo librarian can be a departmental librarian in an organization which may have other librarians, but no other library or information professional working within the department for which he or she is the library *manager*. Or, in the opposite scenario, this person can be the single library or information professional serving the entire organization. The value of the definition is that it recognizes that in his or her immediate workplace this library/information professional works alone, both as a librarian and as a library manager.

Purpose of the book

Managing the New *One–Person Library* is written to provide guidance for the librarian who works with no other professional peers in the immediate organization. If we are to succeed, we and our readers must agree on a basic mission for the one–person library. It is this: Excellence of library service, as achieved through the reconciliation of management for efficiency and commitment for service, is the goal of each one–person librarian. For the proper performance of his or her duties, the successful manager of a one–person library or information service is required to look beyond the immediate tasks of the job and understand that, *in this particular type of information service*, the work produced in the library reflects on the organization or community served, on the users of the library, and on the librarian who is in charge of *managing the facility*. Excellence of service, whether it be delivering a book to the recreational reader in a rural community or providing information in a high-tech scientific research institute, is the reason the librarian is there. This excellence of service, combined with a commitment to the mission of the library and an understanding (and acceptance) of the librarian's accountability in providing library and information service, defines the one–person library manager. This book is written with these concepts in mind.

In bringing forth this book, the authors' goal has been not so much to provide a handbook or 'how–to' manual (although dealing with the basics of librarianship is certainly an important part of this book) but to give the reader a sense of order and direction in the performance of those duties which fall outside the give-and-take of librarians working in larger groups. The success of a one–person library and its services is often a direct reflection of the attitude and personality of the librarian in charge. We have attempted to describe for one–person librarians some of the situations in which they will find themselves and to provide some suggestions on how they might deal with these situations. These efforts should, if we have been successful, give one–person library and information professionals the guidelines and techniques they need for providing excellent service to their users.

Audience

This book is written for any librarian who works alone. Although the book is written for an international readership, we acknowledge that the two authors, one British and one American, are naturally going to present a point of view that will reflect current practices in library management in the United States and the United Kingdom. We have tried to make British concepts understandable to Americans and vice versa, but we recognize that sometimes our familiarity with a situation in one country may cause some confusion on the other. We hope we have avoided the worst pitfalls.

We also have some concern about terms. In the United States, a 'graduate' librarian means someone who has a master's degree in library and information science from a school or university accredited by the American Library Association. In the United Kingdom that person is called a 'chartered' librarian, because the Library Association, which is the accrediting organization, has granted him a charter to serve as a professional librarian. In the United States, a person who runs a single–staff library or information centre is generally called a 'one–person' librarian. In the United Kingdom that person is usually referred to by the acronym 'OMB', which stands for 'one–man–band'. There is, in the United Kingdom, a professional group known as the OMBs, part of Aslib, and the acronym has caught on as a descriptive term. The term cannot be used in this connection in the United States, however, for in America OMB is an acronym for an important government agency (the Office of Management and Budget). The OMB in the United States is often in the news, frequently in areas of concern to librarians and information professionals, so using OMB as a library term would have been confusing for Americans. For that reason, and with apologies to our readers in the United Kingdom, we have chosen to refer to our subject as the 'one-person library' and to its practitioners as 'one-person librarians'.

We have attempted to be uniform about these words and phrases. The 'one–person library', for example, is the term we use to identify any library or information centre within an organization or a community. It can be a unit or department of any kind of firm or organization, or it can be a single–staff public library, either independent or a branch of a larger system. In the case of a public library, when we refer to the parent 'organization' of which the library is a part, we are, of course, referring to the community the library serves and whatever governing authority has responsibility for the support of the library. We acknowledge that a public library's mission might be somewhat different from that of a one–person library in a non–public situation, but it is our belief that the basic principles of management, whether the library serves a public or non–public constituency, are the same, and it is that set of principles we are attempting to offer here. Therefore, when we use the term 'organization' to describe the administrative unit of which the one–person library is a part, we mean either the organization as such, or the community.

Likewise, when we speak of the 'one–person librarian', we are referring to any professional practitioner in the library and information services profession who works alone or, as we have described, with minimal assistance, whether he or she is called a 'one–person' librarian, a 'one–professional' librarian, or a 'solo' librarian. That person can be a single–staff 'information specialist' or other information worker, or an 'information professional'. To us, the words are pretty much interchangeable, and we have used the term 'one–person librarian' to refer to these people.

Thus we have taken care *not* to write this book for librarians in any particular setting but have tried to make reference to the many different kinds of institutions and organizations in which librarians perform their duties. While most one-person librarians seem to work in special libraries, and since many special libraries and information centres are perceived to be connected with business or technical organizations, it might be expected that this book is intended for those in commercial or for-profit firms. This is not the case. As we prepared this text, we became aware that many one–person librarians and information professionals work in small (and sometimes not so small) non–profit or not–for–profit organizations. In fact, many one–person librarians are untrained or unchartered and, as mentioned earlier, many are volunteers. It is hoped that this work will be of particular use to them, as well as to the professional chartered library manager who has not been specially trained to work in a small, one–person unit. Others who will benefit from applying the principles set forth in this book will include the untrained non–professional who has been promoted to a position of library or information management, the student who is interested in one–person librarianship, and the entry-level librarian.

One last caveat. The subject of the sex of the practitioner plays an important part in any professional publication, and works on libraries are particularly vulnerable to misunderstanding, for the library and information services profession is made up primarily of women. Nevertheless, despite the fact that our profession is considered by some to be gender-specific, it is our intention to include men who work in the field, and in the interest of fairness we have tried to vary the personal pronouns throughout this book.

Acknowledgements

We are indebted to a great many people who have cooperated in this project. Since *Managing the One–Person Library* was published in 1986, several thousand people have attended our lectures and seminars – for which the book was often the text – and many of these people frequently offered helpful suggestions and comments. We appreciate hearing from these people. We must also recognize that some of this material has, from time to time, appeared in other places. We are frequently called upon to speak on the subject of one–person librarianship, or to contribute a chapter to a book or collection of articles on library management in general, and we have attempted, whenever these materials are mentioned in the text, to provide a proper citation. If, for one reason or another, we have inadvertently duplicated ideas or concepts which have appeared elsewhere and they are not acknowledged, we apologize.

Finally, as we conclude our acknowledgments, we wish to make reference to Aslib and to the Special Libraries Association, for those organizations have played an important role in the development of our work. Aslib has supported the work of the One-Man Bands Group since the early 1980s, and the SLA was the first, and remains the only, American organization which appreciated our conviction that one–person librarians constitute a viable and productive branch of the library and information services profession. It was primarily through the Special Libraries Association that we were able legitimately, so to speak, to recognize the contribution of the one–person librarian in our society, and for that we are grateful to the SLA. The members of the Special Libraries Association are receptive and encouraging to our way of thinking (again, probably because so many of them work alone), and we appreciate that support.

Chapter Two

The one-person librarian: a profile

Until 1986, little had been written about one–person librarianship, and a profile of the one–person librarian was not easy to come by. Today the picture has changed. Nearly ten years of accumulated writing on the subject has been published in *The One–Person Library: A Newsletter for Librarians and Management,* [1] and much material from the first five years of that publication was anthologized in 1990. [2] Joan Williamson has written about educational and training requirements for the one-person librarian [3], and numerous articles on specific aspects of one–person librarianship have appeared in a variety of professional journals. Additionally, many graduate students in library and information science have written theses and term papers with the one–person library as the focus of their work.

Numbers

The first characteristic sought in a population profile is generally a count, but there are difficulties in attempting to determine how many one–person librarians there are. The two usual measuring agencies, the American Library Association and UNESCO, both measure libraries by size down to a minimum that includes staff of three or less, but there is no attempt to measure libraries which are specifically one–person operations (probably because of the difficulty of trying to count part–time staff, unpaid or volunteer staff, etc.). Nevertheless, there have been some attempts to count one–person librarians. The British Library Research and Development Report entitled *Librarianship and Information Work: Job Characteristics,* [4] drawing on the 1972 census carried out by the Department of Education and Science, determined that 32% of library and information units employ one person either full– or part–time. The 1981 census shows that the figure has grown to about 50%, [5] and if the British Library undertakes a 1991 census, it will undoubtedly show an even larger increase in the number of people who manage libraries and information centres alone.

In its 1986 Triennial Survey, the Special Libraries Association added a new category for counting librarians and information specialists: those who supervise no other staff. At first this seemed like a good gauge of how many one–person librarians there might be in special libraries, but there is a drawback. For while that member of the SLA who responded to the survey might indeed be working alone, she might also be an employee of a larger library unit with no supervisory responsibility, who is in fact supervised by someone else. Nevertheless, some of those responding to this category would be one-person librarians, so the numbers can be used to provide a rough estimate, especially since the quick growth of the SLA's new subgroup for one–person librarians has been so dramatic. Of those surveyed, 27% of the American membership recorded that they supervised no other staff, and 24% of the Canadian members grouped themselves in the same category.[6] By the 1991 (by now Biennial) survey, those percentages has increased to 31% and 27% respectively.[7]

Size of the professional associations

As we try to count one–person librarians, we can get some idea of the numbers by looking at the size of the various professional associations and calculating the percentages given above. The Library Association in the United Kingdom, for example, has approximately 25 000 members. Together with Aslib, with a membership of about 2 000 and the Institute of Information Scientists, with a membership of 2 800, these organizations account for the majority of people working in the library and information services profession in the UK. In North America, both the American Library Association, with a membership of some 52 000 librarians, and the Canadian Library Association, with some 4 700 members, include in their memberships large numbers of one–person librarians. The Special Libraries Association, which is roughly comparable with Aslib in the United Kingdom in that its members are generally (but not always) employed in non-traditional library situations, has an international membership of some 13 000 librarians and information specialists, and the American Society of Information Scientists claims approximately 4 000 members.

There are, of course, people in charge of one–person libraries who do not belong to any of these professional bodies. Nevertheless, if we look at the number of other organizations (especially the subject–oriented ones) which might appeal directly to managers of one–person libraries, it is not difficult to conclude that the number of such library and information professionals is very large, even if only some of the members of these organizations work in one–person units. Organizations such as the British Association of Law Libraries, the School Library Association, the Society of Archivists, the Private Libraries Association, the City Information Group, and, in the United States, professional groups such as the Art Libraries Society/North America, the American Association of Law Libraries, the Music Library Association, the Medical Library Association, the National Librarians Association, the Society of American Archivists, the Theatre Library Association, the Western Association of Map Libraries, the Church and Synagogue Library Association include several thousand library and information professionals, so we can conclude that there are a great many one–person librarians, even when we take into consideration the fact that some of these practitioners may hold dual memberships.

One–person librarians enjoy networking with others who do the same kind of work, and since 1986, they have been organizing themselves. Specific groups for one-person librarians, both informal and formal, are numerous, with the two most prominent being the OMB Group of Aslib and the Solo Librarians Division of the Special Libraries Association, both described earlier. Not so well known are the local groups, single-staff librarians who on their own initiative decide to meet occasionally for breakfast or 'brown-bag' lunches. Examples can be found amongst the departmental libraries of a university (such as the group at the University of Michigan, in Ann Arbor, which includes one–person libraries officially part of the university library system as well as affiliated libraries located on or near the campus) and in several of America's larger metropolitan areas. In New York, the private clubs, most of which have one–person libraries, have a group which meets periodically to discuss issues of mutual interest and concern. In San Francisco, the active group of one-person librarians working in engineering and architectural firms has been so successful that it has inspired a second group, employed in other types of organization, who meet regularly. In Toronto, the One–Person Library Support Group, a subunit of the Toronto Chapter of the Special Libraries Association, has existed for several years and continues to play an influential role in the professional lives of its members.

How one–person libraries come about

There are probably as many reasons why there are one–person libraries as there are organizations and communities that support them. Most, however, would seem to have come about through one of four situations:

- *Incorporated need.* For some types of institutions and organizations, a library or information centre is required from the very beginning, in order to provide information and research services for those who will be working in or using the facility. For example, a group of physicians organizing a clinic in order to concentrate their various practices in one location will include a library or information service in the initial planning. Similarly, those responsible for the design and organization of a new school in the community will incorporate a school library or media centre into the project. Both groups may plan, from the beginning, to have one person in charge of managing the library.

- *Discovered need.* An organization, usually a small company or firm in which a certain amount of information or research is accumulated in the general course of business, will discover that much time is lost in tracking down various items in different offices. A decision will be made to organize books, periodicals, research reports, and similar materials – perhaps combining them with an office in which online searches can be performed - and a library or information centre is established. Such one–person libraries and information centres frequently spring up in architectural or engineering firms, publishing companies or professional and trade associations.

- *Negative need.* There are, alas, those situations where the one–person library operation comes about in unfortunate circumstances, when an organization decides that it cannot afford the services of a team of librarians and staff are let go, with the final result that the library or information service is managed and services are delivered by one person. The unit already exists as part of the organizational structure, but now there is only one person left to do the work formerly assigned to two or more employees. This situation is the most difficult one–person library assignment of all, for what has gone before has created a standard which will be practically impossible to maintain and, no matter how well intentioned the surviving employee is, there is little he can do to prevent a deterioration in the care of the collection or the quality of service.

- *Minimal need.* Some organizations do not need more than minimal library service. There are those situations where only a small library is called for, and while it would be unfair to refer to these libraries as 'static,' the size of the organization they serve simply does not warrant a larger library. Examples of such libraries will be found in law offices, where there are only two or three partners with a receptionist/secretary, and there is very little actual legal research to be done, particularly if the partners themselves are adept at online searching or other forms of research. Similarly, a very small hospital in a rural community will not need a team of librarians to serve the physicians and other hospital staff, and the hospital will engage a single library employee (or participate in a team-service approach in which a 'circuit-riding' librarian visits the hospital on a scheduled basis).

Many of these small libraries and information centres have been organized in the last decade or so to meet the information needs of various user groups. A high proportion of work in these small units calls for generalists and all-rounders; the need for functional specialists, for bibliographers and cataloguers, is basically limited to larger library units, although most one–person librarians do have some sort of subject degree or qualification, depending on the kind of work performed in the parent organization.

Duties and job satisfaction

In the one–person library the work will include everything, from the most senior management tasks to the most menial, and any attempt to divide duties into professional and non–professional, as in larger libraries, would not make much sense. In the variety of tasks to be completed in a day, the well–trained, one–person librarian can also be an educator – to management as well as to staff – and a consultant, teaching non–library staff how to use the library and to make better use of its services. Typically, as the users learn to do more things by themselves, the librarian is able to pursue more challenging tasks.

There are, of course, unpleasant aspects of library work, just as with any job, and the one–person librarian must also perform these tasks. Serjean[5] states that the most unpopular activities in a one–person unit are those associated with clerical and administrative routine. More serious problems may include lack of status, limited time for planning, limited time for professional reading, and lack of further training or personal contact with other professional librarians and information specialists – in sum, frustrated professional development. Hence the establishment of the networking groups mentioned above, with a particularly useful example being the OMB Group of Aslib, a group which effectively cuts across the boundaries of various professional organizations and even includes those who do not qualify for or cannot justify membership of Aslib.

Training

Although discussed in detail in a separate chapter, this profile of the one–person library and information professional should make reference to how these employees are prepared for the work they do. In 1973, according to Serjean, only 38% of staff in one–person operations (in the UK) had subject degrees, and only 31% had professional degrees.[5] By the time of the Williamson study, 15 years later, the picture had changed. More respondents (75%) had library and information qualifications, and almost all had subject degrees or other relevant qualifications.[3] Thus those in charge of hiring information professionals, especially in the one–person situation, seem to have come to the realization that these employees are required to have solid qualifications, whether information-based or not, in order to provide sound library and information services.

Such findings refute the common perception, held until only a few years ago by both lay people and library professionals, that one–person library managers were for the most part non-professional librarians working part-time in small collections serving a minimum number of users. Further refutation came in a survey conducted by OPL Resources Ltd. in the United States and Canada in late 1987. That study determined that fully 70% of all one–person librarians hold a graduate degree in library and information studies, with 83% of OPL's respondents employed full time and serving an average of 66 users each week.[8]

Useful conclusions demonstrating similar attitudes were reached from a study conducted by Janet Shuter and Judith Collins for the British Library Reference Division (BLRD).[9] The content of the study ranged over various aspects of work (including such things as working conditions, qualifications and career history), based on job factors which most came up to the expectations of the employees in single–staff situations. For these people ('the information worker in isolation'), being able to organize one's own time was at the top of the list. The autonomy of the position, the interest level of the work, the fact that tasks requiring specialized and professional or para-professional skills do not have to be delegated, and the variety of the work done in the library all came up to or exceeded their expectations about their work. Other important factors leading to job satisfaction for these one–person librarians included the pleasant situation of being in a position to try out new ideas, being appreciated for their work, and being able to take satisfaction in their work.

Similar findings come up when seminar attendees are asked why they like working in a one–person library environment, but the order is somewhat different. Independence in managing the facility is at the top of the list, followed closely by an appreciation of the responsibility the position entails. The diversity of duties in a one-person library and the possibility of a flexible task schedule – being able to set one's own priorities – is an important positive quality for being a one-person librarian/information professional. The opportunity to learn from the queries coming into the library or information centre is a major attraction for many, as is the level of feedback and appreciation from users when their needs have been satisfactorily met. Similarly, the close involvement with users is considered an advantage of working in a one–person library or information centre, and the challenge of the work, combined with the opportunity for creative problem solving, are all considered important assets.

When asked what they dislike about their work, the problems listed by seminar attendees usually fall into two categories: lack of time and professional isolation. Shuter and Collins found different results, and the factors which their participants regarded as the 'worst' aspects of the job are of interest. For the one–person librarians responding to the survey, lack of training was considered the main problem, followed by such things as reliability (or lack of it) of management support, not knowing what is going on in the parent organization, physical working conditions, the lack of interest (presumably by management) in contributing to personal development, and low pay. Other issues which troubled these librarians included concern about fair company policy and administration, lack of agreement with organizational objectives, job security, physical working conditions, and, again, not knowing what is going on in the parent organization.

It is interesting to note that in the Shuter/Collins study, two positive aspects cited by the group – interest and variety – relate to the content of the job, while dissatisfactions relate mainly to working conditions. This distinction is interesting. Similar trends can be taken from the informal studies of the seminar attendees. Are the most satisfied one–person librarians more motivated because they have better status etc. as a result of performing more interesting tasks, regardless of the working conditions? Or do they attain better status because they are more motivated and market the services of the library better? Which comes first?

For those one–person librarians who are dissatisfied with their work, it is possible to establish a variety of reasons. Two seem sufficiently important to warrant comment. It might not be unfair to suggest that perhaps library schools, despite the efforts of some well-intentioned faculty members, are somewhat at fault for producing the wrong type of graduate to enter the one–person or minimal–staff library field. There seems to be something anomalous in library education – many schools are still educating students to be library managers in charge of several staff, and these students are not prepared when they are thrown into a professional situation where they are expected to do everything. The market indicates that schools should really be training at least some of the students to become all-rounders – bright, adaptable, trainable, able to innovate and cooperate, and with good social skills. Many one–person libraries need entrepreneurs, not bookish and introverted subject specialists. They need to be dedicated, professionally motivated, adaptable and keen, and must not mind a little drudgery at times. Personal development and growth can be as important as academic training, and we should expect the graduate schools of library and information studies to develop these traits in their students. When this area becomes part of the graduate programme those students who accept employment in the one–person library field will find more career opportunities and be less threatened by economic fluctuations. It is an area of graduate education that is being addressed, but more work needs to be done.

A second reason for dissatisfaction in the one–person library can be ascribed to the lack of opportunity for career advancement. Generally speaking, if one wishes to move up in the parent organization, the one–person library is not the place from which to begin the climb. Career advancement from the smaller library and information unit is virtually impossible unless the employee is prepared to move away from purely library and information work into administrative or general management. For the ambitious one–person library or information professional, it might be possible, if there is a demand for increased services, to 'empire–build' and thus create a two– or three–person library operation, but such career advancement is not typical in most one–person library situations. The management decision to have a library or information centre is just that, a management decision, and while the single–staff library manager can influence the direction of information services in the organization, the decision to enlarge (or indeed, reduce) staff size in the library is the responsibility of management, not of the person providing the service.

In addition to the characteristics described so far, the survey by OPL

Resources Ltd. brought forward several other useful facts.[8] Essentially a salary survey, the questionnaire sought to establish reasons for the low pay scale for one–person librarians (about 8% lower than that of other librarians at the time of the survey). Several became apparant. For one thing, the population surveyed was overwhelmingly female (93%), which, when compared to the profession at large (depending on who does the answering – , between 79% and 86% female) is very specific. The one–person branch of library and information management is definitely gender-specific.

The OPL survey revealed another interesting fact with respect to salaries and compensation: about half of all one-person librarians are in the relatively early stages of their library careers, having worked for less than 10 years as librarians. In any profession starting salaries are, of course, relatively low, and these low figures are reflected in the overall average for single-staff librarians. This situation must also be considered in combination with the fact that a sizeable proportion of one–person librarians do not change jobs readily. That is, 26% of all respondents to the OPL survey indicated that they were still working at the same job in which they originally started. Since changing jobs is often the only way to make a sizeable increase in salary, it appears that many one-person librarians, by staying in the same job, are locking themselves into a situation where they can expect little more than standard percentage raises. Since these percentages will generally be based on a fairly small sum to begin with, the overall growth in salary is slow at best.

It was further noted in the OPL survey that the majority of one-person librarians work for organizations with relative small budgets for library services. Indeed, 76% of all respondents worked in libraries with annual budgets (excluding salaries) under $50 000 (in 1988) and for 43% the budgets were under $20 000. Clearly, in organizations where, for whatever reasons, the financial commitment to the library is small, the librarian's salary is likely to reflect that lack of monetary support and be low as well.

In addition to examining why one-person librarians have a lower average salary than other librarians, the OPL survey looked at those factors which appeared to be of greatest significance in maximizing the salaries of one–person librarians. Education, for example, was seen as a major influence. Without exception, all other factors excluded, the higher the level of non-library education, the higher the salary. Those one–person librarians claiming only a secondary education earned a salary 25% below the overall average, and 37% below those boasting a non-library doctoral degree. If non–library education was important, the achievement of a graduate degree in library and information science had an even greater effect on salary. At all levels of education, those with a graduate degree in library and information studies earned significantly more than those without.

In the final analysis, probably the only real way to characterize the one–person librarian is to go to each one and ask him or her to express an opinion about working alone. The authors, in their survey, found that 60% of those asked see themselves as working primarily in public services; that is, providing library and information services to an identified core group of users. The other 40% consider themselves to be primarily technical services personnel, which says something about their view of themselves as information providers. Perhaps for this 40%, their role is not to provide services but to manipulate, organize and store data. If that is the case, in these libraries and information centres where they are the only information employee, it is not a very healthy concept, and serious attempts should be made to change their orientation.

On the other hand, perhaps the glass is half full, for more than half of those who work in one–person situations see themselves as employed to serve their users, or at least employed to facilitate getting the appropriate information or material to the users. They are, indeed, service oriented and expect to be part of the team which supports the parent organization's or the community's goals.

This, then, is perhaps as good an informal portrait of the one-person librarian as can be painted at present. The strength of one–person librarianship is in its diversity, in the fact that so many people, using the same basic procedures and pursuing the same goals, work in so many different environments and with such a variety of subjects and users. At the same time, this diversity leads to a very positive conclusion to this profile of the one-person librarian: the future looks good.

The reasons are not hard to find. Considering the advances in modern technology and the reluctance of contemporary management personnel to add staff to library and information units, it is unlikely that the proportion of one-person librarians will decline. In fact, it is probably safe to assume that it will continue to grow, as management comes to realize that one excellent, efficient and enthusiastic librarian or information specialist is preferable to two or more who do not provide the same level of service. For the one–person librarian who is willing to do the work, there is a very promising future ahead.

References

1   *The One–Person Library: A Newsletter for Librarians and Management.* New York: OPL Resources Ltd., Murray Hill Station PO Box 948, New York, NY 10156, 1984–

2   Berner, Andrew and St. Clair, Guy (eds), *The Best of OPL: Five Years of* The One-Person Library, Special Libraries Association, Washington, DC, 1990.

3   Williamson, Joan, *One–Person Libraries and Information Units: Their Education and Training Needs,* MCB University Press, Bradford, 1988.

4   Serjean, R., 'Librarianship and information work: job characteristics and staffing needs', British Library R&D Report 5321 HC, London, 1973.

5   East, Harry, 'Changes in the staffing of UK special libraries and information services in the decade 1972–1981: a review of the DES census data', *Journal of Documentation*, 39, (4), 1983, 247–265.

6   SLA Triennial Salary Survey 1986, Washington DC, Special Libraries Association, 1986, p. 32.

7   SLA Biennial Salary Survey 1991, Washington DC, Special Libraries Association, 1991, p. 33.

8   'A new survey: salaries and other data', *The One–Person Library: A Newsletter for Librarians and Management*, 5, (4), August 1988, p. 2.

11   Shuter, J. and Collins, J., 'The isolated professional', *Information and Library Manager*, 3, (4), 1984, 106.

Chapter Three

Professional isolation and independence

There are advantages to working in a small library, and a one–person situation offers even more attractive advantages. Certainly for those who prefer
working independently the independence can be a very special inducement
for providing first–class work, an opportunity many in the workforce do not
have. When one–person librarians are asked to name the best thing about
their work – the one thing they would not change – the answer invariable
has to do with their independence. Yet these same people, when asked to
comment about the worst part of one–person librarianship, give the same
answer or a variation of it: 'professional isolation'. It would appear that
these characteristics of one–person librarianship are two sides of the same
coin. What can be done to alleviate the problem of isolation while enhanc-
ing the benefits of independence?

Advisors

The answer depends very much on the personality of the librarian, and his
or her willingness to seek out others who may be in a position to advise,
consult, discuss and/or simply listen to the problems and pleasures of
one–person librarianship. Occasionally, of course, there is someone on the
staff of the parent organization or in the community who is in a position to
listen, a co–worker, perhaps, or a supervising management person, or a
user who enjoys the library and spends much time there. Possibly even a
member of the committee or board which plays a role, advisory or supervisory, in the library's management can be one who comes to the library as
much to listen as to work. Similarly, many librarians find that as they have
reached a certain point in their careers, they have acquired, either formally
or informally, a mentor who takes an advisory role in their professional situation, and these people, too, can be valuable to the one–person librarian. If
there is such a person, the wise librarian will go to him or her occasionally
to seek advice, to inform, and certainly to share some of the more theoreti-
cal and problematic questions that come up from time to time in running
the library. This kind of involvement on the part of interested people is certainly good public relations, probably second only to the quality of service
provided, in encouraging people to think positively about the library and its
services.

There are dangers, however, and the lay person, no matter how interested he or she might be in the workings of the library, can only advise from the point of view of a non–professional. The lay person, despite the best intentions, is not qualified to understand many of the one–person librarian's concerns. Also, the lay person, particularly if he or she is a user of the library or information centre, a member of the committee that advises on library policy, or even another employee in the organization who takes an interest in the library, is more likely than not to have his or her own agenda for the library and for decisions made about the library. In this case, the librarian can, quite rightly, be concerned about the advisor's objectivity. In professional matters, it is in the librarian's best interest – and that of the community or the parent organization – to seek advice elsewhere.

Other professionals

So we look to other professionals for advice, but in the one–person library, how do we do this? Communication plays a vital role here, for the librarian who works alone has no one to turn to for professional concerns except other librarians, often others who also work alone, but just as often librarians and information professionals who work in larger institutions with whom the one–person librarian shares common interests and concerns. It is through setting up lines of communication with other librarians that we find a solution to the problems of professional isolation.

There are several ways in which the one–person librarian can seek out other librarians with whom to associate, and the route to those associations can very often be the same independence which he or she has identified as the prime advantage of working in the single–staff situation. The librarian who works alone is, of course, on the job for most of the work shift, and one of the problems of this situation is the difficulty of getting away to meet with others or to attend professional meetings and seminars. On the other hand, one of the advantages of working alone is the opportunity the librarian has of setting up the work patterns, managing time and arranging the routines in such a way that, when possible, he or she benefits from the schedule. Although there are certain duties that must be performed at fixed times, there are others that are more flexible and it is these duties that the librarian who works alone arranges and rearranges to suit his or her own schedule. Even the librarian who is unable to get away from the office for outside meetings can arrange some of the duties to make time to talk to others on the telephone.

So if the primary advantage of managing a one–person library is the independence of the librarian, how can that independence be used for his professional benefit of the librarian? How can the independence of the one–person librarian be used to open the lines of communication with other librarians? There are three possibilities:

- professional associations
- personal contacts
- connections and networking

Each plays a different role in the professional life of the one–person librarian, yet each is vital to the successful functioning of the library or information centre which is his or her responsibility.

Professional associations

For librarians and information professionals, especially those who work alone, professional associations not only have a practical value - they affirm one as a professional. Ferguson and Mobley assert that 'one important mark of a profession is that it has an organization addressed to its concerns', and they characterize membership in a professional organization as 'vital' in developing a professional career.[1] It is through his affiliation with a professional organization that the manager of a library or information centre is accepted, in the parent organization or the community, as a professional practitioner of his profession. Just as practitioners in law, medicine, theology, education, the arts, and even the business community, are regarded as 'professional' practitioners because they are affiliated with their respective professional organizations, so too are librarians and information specialists acknowledged as professionals in their field when they are affiliated with their recognized professional organizations.

There is a variety of organizations connected with the library and information services profession (many of which were mentioned in the previous chapter) and each of them exists to play a particular role in the professional lives of working librarians. If a professional association is properly fulfilling its mission to its membership, it should be offering the following support services:

- education and training
- meetings and conferences
- subject or special–interest affiliations within the larger organization
- geographical and/or local chapters
- a register of members
- research programmes
- information services
- publications

The wise librarian, especially the one–person library manager, will take advantage of the opportunity to belong to several such groups, even if participating equally in the activities of each of the associations is not possible (and it seldom will be).

The benefits of membership are numerous, and not to be taken lightly by the practising professional. The most obvious, of course, is the professional literature, for every organization has a journal (some have more than one) which comes across the librarian's desk with increasing – and occasionally alarming – frequency. One of the most common complaints for most librarians is that there is too much professional literature. For some this may be the case, but for others, the literature which comes with professional memberships is an important part of their professional growth and development. Those who have mastered time–management techniques and are comfortable with scanning the contents pages find much useful material in their journals. They simply file a mental reference to read a particular article at a more relaxed time, and at the same time they have a general idea of the contents of the journal. The librarian managing a small, single–person library or information centre, interested in knowing what is going on in the profession and appreciating that there will be new developments, new technologies and different approaches to library management, will find much of value in the literature emanating from his or her professional organizations.

So while these organizations provide a wealth of materials and many services for the one–person librarian, there are other advantages to belonging to such professional groups. In addition to professional affirmation, library associations provide members with the opportunity to interact with one another – probably the most important asset a professional association may offer for those librarians who will take advantage of them. Certainly the one–person librarian who can justify the time and can do the work should get appointed to committees, participate in workshop planning groups, present papers, and so forth. Frankly, if one is serving in some capacity in a professional association, management is more likely to accede to a request for participation. This does not, however, imply that one must be a 'doer' in order to benefit from membership in an organization. Serving on committees and boards and task forces is not the primary objective of most people who join professional groups. If one does become involved, so much the better for the organization, but as long as the dues are paid, one does not have to feel guilty if one merely attends meetings and reads the journals. It is not written anywhere that active participation is the only way to benefit from belonging to a professional association.

However, there is a more practical side which should be considered. If the one–person librarian recognizes the advantages of belonging to a professional organization – going out to meet people, attending conferences and seminars, visiting other libraries to see how they are managed etc., – how does one go about it?

First of all, management must be convinced that it is for the benefit of the parent organization or the community for the one–person librarian to participate. In any business or profession, the better informed the employee is, the better employee he or she will be, so it becomes the librarian's obligation to discuss frankly and openly the advantages of membership for the employer. The object is to persuade management to support the librarian's participation with a commitment of funds and release time, and to assess the benefits that such activities will bring to the parent organization or community.

If management is receptive to the idea of some professional participation for the one-person librarian, it is better to treat each meeting separately rather than to seek a blanket absence, such as suggesting that one must be away at a certain time each year for a particular conference. Since supervising personnel can be better informed about the specific advantages of each meeting if permission is requested separately, the librarian is not perceived as putting attendance at the meeting before the subject matter.

On the other hand, for the one–person librarian who is entering into negotiations for a position, it is wise to indicate from the beginning that participation in professional activities is important, and to state what one's expectations are as far as travel, release time and financial support are concerned. Most managers who hire library and information professionals are willing to include such considerations if they understand early on in the relationship how the parent company or organization will benefit, and in the larger scheme of things they will recognize that it is to the employer's benefit to make these concessions in order to hire the best candidate for the position.

In addition to management support and approval, there are other practical considerations in the one–person librarian's participation in professional activities. One, of course, is the scheduling of meetings and events. It is difficult for the one–person librarian to get away during business hours, but most professional groups seem to try to plan at least some of their meetings and programmes in the evenings and/or at weekends, and in the US there is now a trend to schedule breakfast meetings, making attendance more convenient for those who manage their libraries and information centres without additional staff.

The librarian working in a one–person library or information centre needs to know what is happening in the profession, at the local, regional, national and international levels, and membership in professional associations provides this information. While the benefits of membership in international organizations might seem to be limited for the one–person library manager, in fact that librarian can bring much to the successful performance of her duties by belonging to such organizations. The librarian, for example, who works in a small anthropological museum, connected with a university, will find great benefit in belonging to an international library organization that has a subject group related to her work, either in the area of museum library management or in the specific area of library services in anthropological studies. In other words, even if she cannot attend the international conferences, belonging to the organization, reading the literature and keeping abreast of developments puts her in a position to provide a better service to her users.

In order to provide that excellence of service referred to earlier, the one–person librarian needs to be able to relate to trends in the profession, to know what thinking is being done about the future of the profession, and how his or her work will be affected. Membership in a national organization will usually bring information about both national and international issues, and at the local or regional level, library groups provide not only information about what is happening closer to home, but also professional support in the form of opportunities for informal networking.

Interpersonal networking and connections

The discussion of the role of professional associations for the one–person librarian leads directly to a consideration of personal contacts, for it is in the professional associations that we first become acquainted, and perhaps even friendly, with the people we want to know when we need to call upon them. It is not at all uncommon for librarians and other information professionals, gathering for a meeting, to have a few minutes to socialize before the programme begins, and it is in those few minutes that we can make the personal contacts which can be so useful. Librarians do not necessarily have to go to one another's libraries to interact profitably; their friendships, developed from casual meetings at professional gatherings, can lead to confidence about ringing up when they have a question to ask or another's opinion to seek.

This is why such groups are usually defined as interpersonal networks, to distinguish them from the more formal, contractual arrangements entered into between the libraries themselves. Any library and information professional is already part of an interpersonal network, which Beth Wheeler Fox defined most simply in 1988:

> Do you ever each lunch with a neighboring librarian or call with a question...? If so, you have just created an informal network. Librarians routinely need to know how to resolve an enormous variety of questions. Quick answers are rarely available. A search through library literature would provide many answers, yet the item in shortest supply is time.... Networking allows us to share this type of knowledge with one another.[2]

Interpersonal networks come with several distinctive characteristics, which were identified by Edward G. Strable in 1980 and which are particularly relevant for the manager of a one–person library. For one thing, according to Strable, these interpersonal networks are not really 'organized' but just 'come into being'; one doesn't join but just sort of melds into the network after a period of apprenticeship which can vary in length; there are no written rules ('although codes of conduct are severe, automatically sensed, and carefully adhered to by all' members of the group); illegal and unethical methods are not used; and most important, the product of these networks is 'usually' information. Strable also found that, 'in the exchange of information, the similarity to the 'old boy network' is very apparent'.[3]

The concept has been considered before in connection with special librarianship, but it is equally applicable to any library or information centre which is managed by one person:

> It is in the similarity to the 'old boy/old girl' networks that interpersonal networking is most effective. But where the term 'old boy' carries dangerously elitist connotations, the concept is actually preeminently egalitarian. In the information profession, literally anyone has the potential to be an 'old boy' or an 'old girl' Rather than lean on past or inherited relationships –school, professors, and so forth – special librarians have the opportunity to make virtually every colleague a new link in a chain of resources. If professional success is defined in terms of excellence of service – really the only criterion appropriate to describe professional success – does it not follow that whatever efforts and techniques employed, including shared information communicated in the personal relationships with colleagues, are appropriate for the attainment of that excellence?[4]

Such interpersonal networks are really no more than connections, and the idea of using them in achieving excellence in library and information services is not a new one. It was, however, given new impetus and a sort of formalization a few years ago when Carol Nemeyer, Associate Librarian of Congress for National Programs, used it as the theme during her term of office as President of the American Library Association.[5] Nemeyer was discussing how more formal connections (with the business community, for example, or the heads of state library agencies) can be useful to the profession as a whole, but her theme inspires us to look at what connections we can use. When one seeks connections one simply observes which people or organizations may be useful in one's work, and when the need arises they are approached. If a user needs to see a particular type of material not collected at one's own library, for example, but the one–person librarian has been recently introduced to another librarian who does collect the needed material, it is far simpler for the user, and for the parent organization or community employing the librarian, to be put in touch with the librarian who has the material. It is not a complicated idea, and it is certainly one which most exploit from time to time, but it is something which should be considered as a regular resource for the innovative librarian. Connections can make our lives much easier, and certainly improve the results for our users.

Connections lead to cooperation, and for successful one–person librarians who share a vision of what library service can be for their users and for the organizations and communities that employ them, the results can be beneficial for all concerned. Michael Gorman recognized this new trend in 1986, positing that 'libraries and cooperation cannot be separated', since cooperation is 'not an activity librarians may or may not choose to engage in'. What most people think of as a library, Gorman asserted, is in fact a 'fusion of all libraries through cooperation'. He also sought, in a concept that makes notable sense for the manager of a one–person library, to define the 'library' from the library user's point of view, since 'to any library user, the question is not a building, or a collection, or an administrative structure': It is 'are the materials and services available to me when I need them?' Gorman advocated returning library service to the 'local and small units favored by library users', and suggested 'selflessness' as the new ethic of librarianship, stating that 'Selflessness in librarianship would not only be 'right' but also would be of practical benefit – to librarians, individual libraries, and most importantly, to the users of libraries'.[6]

One–person library managers are in a naturally advantageous position as far as cooperative arrangements are concerned, for small size, the limitations of collections, and the uniqueness of some of the problems are typical characteristics that lead to professional collaboration, according to Herbert S. White.[7]

It is just such participation in networking arrangements, particularly in multitype networks, that is especially valuable to managers of one–person libraries, according to Joan S. Segal:

> As difficult as it is for these librarians to find the time to take part in networking activities, just as important is their participation in the wider world of library development. With little or no opportunity for professional development in librarianship in their work environment, network participation with librarians in other ... types of libraries presents an invaluable method for maintaining and updating one's professional competencies.[8]

Formal networks

Because they are joined, usually at some cost to the parent organization or community of which the one–person library is a part, and because their utilization must be justified in terms of value for money, formal networks require a different kind of consideration. 'That no library and information service can be self-sufficient, but needs to become involved in the exploitation of shared resources, has been an established fact since the early 1930s.'[9] This quotation from Burkett (1982) describes the philosophy in many libraries in the United Kingdom, and the picture in the United States is not much different: 'Libraries ... take pride in cooperating well with one another ... No librarians think of their resources as limited to their own institutions'.[10]

In the United States, networks are officially defined by the US National Commission on Libraries and Information Science (NCLIS): 'Two or more libraries and/or other organizations engaged in a common patter of information exchange, through communication, for some functional purpose. A network usually consists of a formal arrangement whereby materials, information and services provided by a variety of libraries and/or other organizations are made available to potential users'.[11]

It is commonly accepted within the profession that networking is still evolving, but for the one–person librarian there are many useful networks. These are often affiliated with a regional library system or a group of libraries within an industry or corporation, and formal participation in such networks provides such benefits to the one–person library as the free exchange of photocopies, hand–delivered interlibrary loans and other document delivery services, cooperative acquisitions projects (wherein the network will purchase materials too costly for one library to purchase alone, and all participants in the network will have access to the materials), last-resort reference services (for queries which cannot be answered in any individual member library), continuing education programs, shared consultation services, and similar programmes. Some networks are more useful than others, often depending on the quality of materials available, but generally speaking, participation in such networks is advantageous to the single–staff library manager.

The larger and more sophisticated the network, the more the one–person library and its users will benefit from the relationship. Many in the profession acknowledge that the primary advantage of participation in formal networking activities is the access they provide to additional resources, thus enabling the library or information unit to have more resources available for meeting its users' needs, and this is particularly true if the network is a multitype one. Without question, formalized networking arrangements benefit the one–person library manager, enabling him or her to approach, with some serious chance of success, that excellence of service that is the library's stated goal.

References

1   Ferguson, Elizabeth and Mobley, Emily R., *Special Libraries at Work*, Library Professional Publications, an imprint of The Shoe String Press, Inc., Hamden, Connecticut: 1984, p.161.

2   Fox, Beth Wheeler. *The Dynamic Community Library: Creative, Practical and Inexpensive Ideas for the Director*. American Library Association, Chicago, Illinois: 1988, p. 19

3   Strable, Edward G. 'The way it was,' in *The Special Library Role in Networks*. ed. Robert W. Gibson, Special Libraries Association, New York, 1980.

4   St. Clair, Guy, 'Interpersonal networking: it is who you know', *Special Libraries*, 80, (2), Spring, 1989, p. 108.

5   'President Nemeyer: Seeking good connections [1982 ALA Annual Conference Inaugural Address]' *American Libraries*, 13, (9), 1982, p. 531.

6   Gorman, Michael, 'Laying siege to the fortress library: a vibrant technological web connecting resources and users will spell its end'. *American Libraries*, 17, (5), 1986, p. 325 – 328.

7   White, Herbert S, *Managing the Special Library*. Knowledge Industry Publications, Inc., White Plains, NY: 1984, p. 113.

8   Segal, Joan S. 'Special libraries and multitype networks,' *Special Libraries*, 80, (2), Spring 1989, p. 91.

9   Burkett, J., 'Library and information networks', *Handbook of Special Librarianship and Information Work*, Aslib, London, 1982, p. 377.

10 Benson, Joseph, 'Networking: the new wave for special librarians,' *Special Librarianship: A New Reader*, The Scarecrow Press, Metuchen, New Jersey, 1980, p. 380.

11 Rouse, William B. and Rouse, Sondra H., *Management of Library Networks: Policy Analysis, Implementation and Control*, New York: Wiley, 1981, pp. 4-5.

Chapter Four

Training and continuing education for the one-person librarian

There has been a growing emphasis in recent years on continuing education and training in all areas of industry and commerce. Both public and private sectors have been admonished for neglecting it.[1] Indeed this report produced by the National Economic Development Council (NEDC) states that in Germany, the USA and Japan, the effect of the recession has been to increase both the number of trainees and the amount spent by firms on vocational training. Unfortunately, in the UK, training is rarely seen as an investment, and a report by Coopers and Lybrand[2] found that regrettably, training is often treated as an overhead which can be cut when profits are under pressure, or as something forced on the company as a reaction to other developments. Another report, prepared by the Open University[3] urges that lifelong learning is important in order to equip people to cope with rapid social, economic and technical change. At the same time in the United States, Darlene Weingard was warning that qualifications 'whether they be academic, vocational or technical, have an average shelf-life of only five years'. [4] The Association of American Library Schools was also concerned that 'continuing library education is one of the most important problems facing librarianship today.' [5]

Before proceeding further with the training needs of one-person librarians, we should look at the definitions of training, and education, as the use of these terms in different contexts often causes difficulties.

Formal training and education – clarification of terms

What is the difference between 'education' and 'training'? How do we define the different types of education? Why is training needed? In her report on investment in training, [6] Margaret Slater uses the following definitions:

1. *Vocational education*. Typically leading to a qualification of some kind, usually from a library/information school, but in the UK, City and Guilds certificates and the chartering process also belong in this category.

2. *Continuing education*. Tops up the previous process over a working lifetime, so that the original professional education does not become obsolete.

3. *System, service and task-related training*. This fits the trainee to the particular job held, to the particular context in which it is carried out, and the tools of the trade used. Task-related training, it is said, is always the responsibility of the individual employer, not of the formal education system.

4. *Personal professional development*. This connects with an individual's career motivation and needs, and defines and facilitates his or her career path. It may contain elements of vocational and continuing education, but its aim is highly individualistic, concerned with the actualization of a unique package of talents and the fulfilment of personal ambitions and hopes.

Perceived benefits of training and continuing education

It is right to stress at this point the payoffs and bonus effects of training and continuing education. Training pays both directly and indirectly. Perceived direct results include increased efficiency, cost-saving and a job properly done. More oblique benefits include increased motivation – important for a one-person librarian who works alone.

Why do one-person librarians need training and continuing education? Readers will by now have realized that most one-person librarians are the only professionally trained information providers in their organizations. Many have clerical assistance, although this may not be full-time. They are thus often professionally isolated within their own organizations. In this situation, continuing education is vital in order to make contact and network with other professionals who have the same sort of problems and training needs. One-person librarians also need to be exposed to new developments which could help them in their library and thus avoid professional stagnation. Personal development is also very important for one-person librarians in order to maintain motivation. They also need help in order to sustain arguments and cases for career status and enhancement. Good time management is essential when working alone. Last, but by no means least, knowing 'how to manage your boss'[7] is vital as most one-person librarians report to a superior who has no information management qualifications.

In a study of the further education and training needs of one-person librarians, Joan Williamson[8] looked at the variety of work performed by these people in their information units. It was found that one well-trained and well-organized information professional was a considerable asset to the organization. It should be possible to demonstrate that by improving the appropriate management and interpersonal skills, and hence the ability to liaise with management, one-person librarians will be better placed to sell the value of information. By so doing they can raise the profile of the information unit, and hence their own status within the organization. It can thus be proved that training really does pay.

One-person librarians therefore need to do three things if they are concerned about keeping on top of their jobs:

1. Assess the areas in which you may need further training and/or continuing education and professional development. List these in order of priority, especially if the training budget is small. Some training needs have already been identified – others will become evident later in this chapter.

2. Look at the many different courses and packages available. Which gives best value for money? Is the course format suitable? How much time can be spared to attend? Who is organizing the course or providing the training? Details of some suitable courses are given later.

3. Make a case for management convincing him/her that you need to participate in continuing education and training courses.

Library school education and working alone

In the survey carried out by Williamson,[8] library school education was not felt by many one-person librarians to be very satisfactory. Many declared that the curriculum did not deal adequately with issues relating to special libraries, and quite a number found themselves unprepared for working alone. They felt that the subjects taught in library and information schools also needed to give due regard to the special library situation, for that is where many one-person librarians are found. In addition, a new market in information skills is emerging, which demands skills in statistics, information retrieval, office automation, and expert systems, amongst others. Nearly all respondents voiced a need for more information technology skills. To be fair, library schools in both the US and the UK are now trying to incorporate more of these topics into their curricula and have been complimented for helping to banish computer illiteracy in the profession. However, curriculum revision takes time and changes need to be validated. The timescale for change is therefore in years rather than months.

Some of the respondents in Margaret Slater's report for the British Library[6] felt the same way. She quotes the head of a library and information school as saying, 'Cloistered education on its own is unreal and has to be backed up by experience. It can only be good in certain respects. For instance, information technology can be learned perfectly well by an IT buff sitting on his butt alone in a library school, but you can't learn to be a good, person-directed information worker there. That has to be learned amongst people in a real [information] service, out in the real world'.

Educational background of one-person librarians

Before making any further suggestions about the continuing education needs of one-person librarians, it might be wise to look at their educational backgrounds. Various surveys in the UK have shown that the educational backgrounds of these information workers are not uniform. In the Williamson survey,[8] which is the one most recently carried out, a quarter of the respondents lacked formal library/information qualifications. However, all but one of these had other qualifications gained during a period of higher education. Those who are qualified in information work do not necessarily have the same qualifications. Many had a first degree in another discipline, followed by a post-graduate qualification in information work. Others had a joint honours degree or a first degree in information work. Some had gone on to take a master's degree or even a doctorate, but usually in a discipline other than information work. To complicate matters even further, in the UK not all library and information-trained respondents were chartered members of the Library Association, but most belonged to at least one of the professional associations. Thus there are many factors about educational background to take into account when providing continuing education and training programmes. Library schools, professional associations and commercial training organizations need to be made aware of these. Thankfully, they are becoming aware that posts in small special libraries and information units are on the increase, as are posts in non-traditional areas such as information management.

The training needs of non-library qualified one-person librarians

Professionals who are not formally qualified as librarians may need training in those skills normally taught at library school. Surprisingly perhaps, some of those interviewed in the Williamson survey thought basic library skills unnecessary, and in common with the respondents who were library school-eduated, felt that such skills as using the new technology, information sources, communications skills and personal development were far more important. However, it may have been difficult for that sample of information workers to make an impartial judgement on the need for basic library and information skills, for the very reason that they lack formal information qualifications: they may well not realize that they need basic library skills! However, some did remark on their lack of such skills and the comments of one such graduate one-person librarian may well sum up the case for obtaining relevant training: 'I regret not having some library/information qualifications now that I am on my own... I lack some background knowledge and [consequently] have some difficulty in trying to convince my organization of the need for further resources'.

Induction training

Many one-person librarians receive no induction training, either for the post held or in order to become more familiar with their organization. This reflects adversely on employers, but is not surprising given the current climate and attitudes toward training by many employers. In addition, one-person librarians seldom report to another librarian, so this can cause difficulties when their training needs are assessed by non-library trained management. In a smaller organization, induction training could be on a one-to-one basis, but in a larger organization it is usually part of a comprehensive corporate training programme. In whatever form induction training is presented, it is vitally important that one-person librarians become involved as soon as possible for the following reasons:

* Understanding the aims of the parent organization

* Getting to know other staff

* Hearing views other than those of the library/information department

* Getting to know existing/potential users of the library/information service

If, as a newly employed one-person librarian, you are not included in any induction training, *ask* to be included. If your organization does not have an induction course, then suggest that they introduce one, and even offer to teach other staff about what the information unit can do!

Continuing education and training needs

Readers will already be aware that the range of library and information situations in which one-person librarians find themselves is diverse, and a knowledge of many different subjects, disciplines and skills is needed. Because of their work situation and permanent shortage of time, one-person librarians have made it very clear that courses must be relevant to their present job. The six most important areas in which further training is seen to be needed are:

* Using new technology

* Information sources

* Communication skills

* Information retrieval

* Personal development

* Evaluation of user needs

There are also many other areas where skills are needed and these include library management and library administration, non-book media, research methods, financial management, and networking. Those who do not have specialist subject degrees might need more training in their subject areas.

We have seen that there are many factors that should motivate one-person librarians to seek out relevant courses and attend them. Among these are:

- Self-awareness and desire to update existing professional skills

- Need for better time management

- Personal development and improved motivation

- Learning a new skill (e.g. searching a online database, or mastering skills not taught at library school, such as communications or customer care)

- Improved status

There must be many others and all one-person librarians should regularly review their training and continuing education needs. Fortunately, there now exist courses specially developed for one-person librarians, and it is suggested that attendance at one of these would be very useful once the librarian is established in his or her post.

Courses specially developed for the one-person librarian

The first organization in the United Kingdom to develop a one-day course especially aimed at the lone information provider was Task Force Pro Libra Ltd. (TFPL). 'On Your Own But Not Alone' is a practical training course on the techniques of 'surviving and thriving' in a one-person library or information unit. The same organization also runs a course on 'Maximizing Your Value to Your Organization' which details the benefits of cooperation and shows how the information professional can be the organization's favourite entrepreneur. There is also an 'instant library' course which tells a one-person librarian all there is to know about setting up a library or information service from scratch. Aslib have followed suit and now also provide a one-day course for one-person librarians which gives advice about setting up and running a one-man band operation.

In the United States, OPL Resources Ltd., a training, consulting and publishing company with offices in New York and Washington, offers seminars of interest to one-person library managers, including basic one- and two-day management courses, a seminar on leadership skills for library managers, a programme on customer services for one-person librarians, and one on advocacy techniques for the one-person library. In addition, other commercial training firms offer occasional management programmes for the one-person librarian.

How to overcome deterrent to training

There are various circumstances which could cause difficulties to someone running his or her own library or information unit. These include:

- Expensive courses

- Relevant subjects not covered

- Badly organized courses

- Long distances to travel

- Difficulty in getting away from a busy information unit

- No recognition of attendance by employers

Firstly, the need to think positively becomes paramount. When working alone, it becomes all to easy to indulge in negative feelings and procrastination. For instance, only a small percentage of one-person librarians have no cover whatsoever for their unit, but the most common excuse for not being able to attend training courses is lack of time and necessary cover for the library. This time factor is often an excuse for laziness and 'doing nothing', because this takes less effort than justifying the need for training. One-person librarians should be prepared to organize their time better and to shoulder some of the responsibility for identifying training needs by seeking out suitable courses for themselves. If a one-person librarian is unsure about a choice of course, then he or she should talk to colleagues, find someone who has been on a similar course and make comparisons about value for money, etc. He or she also needs to make the employer more aware of the benefits of training and the extra impetus that it brings to a job. It is no use assuming that all employers realize this – some have poor training policies and need to be re-educated.

However, it does seem that the message is getting through to one-person librarians. One librarian who works in a one-person library in the commercial field, was recently quoted as saying, 'In a one-man band situation, all training has to be external, and 4 – 5 day courses are out of the question. Training is, however, vitally important for OMBs, and you have got to take responsibility for it, both for your own sake, your own professional development and career, and for that of the [information] service'.

Course format

Course format seems to play a large part in influencing one-person librarians to take part in training programmes. The preferred formats are 'courses held at local training centers' followed by 'a series of talks given by a professional association'. The former obviously dispenses with the need to travel great distances and helps with keeping down the cost. Activities run in-

house did not seem to be popular with one-person librarians, although these presumably would not include induction courses or corporate training on topics such as communication skills or customer care, which would be better run for all staff right across the board, not just information people. 'Distance learning' and 'teach-yourself' programmes also did not seem to be popular, presumably because of the lack of networking possibilities and communication with other one-person librarians. There was also the isolation factor, lack of feedback and working long hours into the evening after a tiring day. Most one-person librarians, when asked, seem to favour short courses of a half- to one-day duration, because of the time factor involved. If a series of these short courses can be linked to provide a module, then so much the better.

Computer assisted learning

There may be a case for more computer assisted learning packages, both for one-person librarians and other library staff. After all, cost is demonstrably an important factor in deterring one-person librarians from participating in further training. Of course, professional bodies and other course organizers must recover their costs, but it should be possible for them to cooperate to offer experimental schemes with computer assisted learning courses, perhaps with the help of acknowledged experts in this field. The initial development of such programmes is expensive, but other costs are saved as no trainer is necessary, programmes can be used repeatedly, and the one-person librarian can fit the training into the schedule whenever it suits, and work at his or her own pace. Computer-assisted learning also cuts out the need to travel, to take time off work, and solves the problem of range and level of skills. The only thing it will not solve is isolation.

For those one-person librarians who are interested, a computer-assisted learning package on time management has been marketed in the United States by the Special Libraries Association and has been well received there; so well received that the SLA soon began to offer other computer-assisted learning courses, all of use to the one-person librarian. Subjects covered include written communications skills, online searching, and marketing, with other programmes scheduled for development. There is no reason why in the UK, some innovative courses could not be offered at local training centres (such as library schools) so that participants can meet together to discuss problems and receive training at the same time.

Responsibility for continuing education and training

Ultimately, this responsibility lies with the one-person librarian. The professional associations, commercial organizations and employers can provide the best training schemes in the world, but if the librarian cannot or will not

make time to attend, their efforts are wasted. One-person librarians who doubt the benefits of training do their more enlightened colleagues no favours either. Moaning about the cost of a course also becomes short-sighted if an inefficient one-person librarian is losing her organization money through poor time-management and the inability to organize her unit properly.

Library and information schools have an important part to play here during initial education. Not only should they be tutoring students in the skills relevant to modern librarianship and information work, but they should be stressing the need for continuing education and for skills to be updated. It has been shown in both the American and UK professional press that the average shelf-life of a degree is no more than 5 years. Library schools might well act as local training centres; the realization of this is dawning, as found in Margaret Slater's report [6] when she quotes a head of a library and information school as saying: 'What we can do best (in university education) is expand students' horizons, not just teach them how to do things. I'm slightly suspicious of professional development as such. It's not just fitting people into slots, nor ego-conscious career grooming. Continuing education – I'm happier with that descriptor. Sooner or later we will have to provide a programme of continuing education for members of the profession from here, but we don't have to do it yet'.

One-person librarians who wish to find out about courses run by departments of information and library management based at universities and polytechnics in the UK can write to the Library Association's Education Department for the brochure *Where to Study in the UK,* or apply directly to the appropriate college. Several library and information science departments have developed management courses at postgraduate and master's level, and some distance learning packages are available. In the United States, information is also available through the various graduate schools of library and information science, and the professional associations (SLA, ALA, ASIS etc.) all maintain professional development/continuing education committees which can advise interested one-person librarians seeking further training.

Courses for non-library trained personnel

The Library Association's pamphlet *Qualification for Library Assistants* gives useful information on courses that will provide the basic library skills needed by some one-person librarians:

- The City and Guilds' library assistants' qualification, which can be taken on either a day-release or distance learning basis. Courses are run by a number of local authority colleges of further education in the UK.

- The Business and Technical Education Council National Awards (B/TEC) in business and finance can now include a double option in library and information work. Again run by some local authority colleges in the UK.

- The National and Higher National Certificates in Library and Information Science are awarded by SCOTVEC – the Scottish Vocational Education Council. Run by various Scottish colleges.

In addition, there are courses for library assistants offered by the Library Association and commercial training organizations such as TFPL in London, which might well meet the needs of non-library trained professionals. TFPL's 'First Steps' course is run as a series of one-day training sessions for persons new to library and information work, and which could be completed individually or, over a period of months, to form a linked module. Subjects include online searching of remote and in-house databases, company information, periodical circulation, general reference work and records filing and management – all skills needed by non-library trained personnel.

Professional Associations in the UK

The professional bodies such as the Library Association, Aslib and the Institute of Information Scientists have an important role to play in encouraging and providing further education for all librarians, not just one-person librarians. Indeed, Aslib and the Library Association are at present the major providers of such courses for the profession in the UK. However, the present provision of continuing education and training by these bodies is felt to be unsatisfactory, not only by such notables as Wilfred Saunders[9] who argues cogently for a more systematic and coordinated approach than that already provided, but by some of the respondents to Margaret Slater's report on training. Taking their views into account, she says, 'At the national level, it was believed that coordination of external training activity in the UK, in order to avoid overlap and wastage, would be beneficial. Exactly how this was to be achieved was not outlined specifically by anyone. Yet it was felt by some that the library and information science professional associations could play an active part in this process. Added to that, some clearer, nationwide agreement on training objectives and means to achieving them would be more than useful. It was necessary to identify 'who we are training for what' roles and purposes. In other words, respondents were hinting at a need for a national training policy for library and information services staff, which would apply to both internal and external training, and link up intelligently with the formal system of vocational education. Thus the present unfocused, uneven and uncoordinated nature of training activity across the board amounts to an issue and indicates lack of commitment'.

This is substantiated by many of the one-person librarians questioned in

the Williamson study. They have indicated that there is a need to provide more relevant courses of suitable length – linked to provide modules – rather than the 'one-off' courses being provided at present. In addition, the costs need to be reasonable, especially in times of reduced training budgets. Professional bodies also need to provide clear and regular information about courses available. At present, in the UK, there is little clear and regular up-to-date listing of the continuing education programmes and short courses available which would be of use to workers in the library and information services field. Journals such as *The LA Record* and *Aslib Information* list courses run by the organizations themselves, as well as those run by groups and commercial organizations in the library and information services field, such as TFPL and the British Library, but they often fail to mention the numerous useful courses run by outside, non-library organizations such as the Industrial Society, British Institute of Management or the many online hosts. To add to the confusion, it is doubtful whether one-person librarians who are not members of the professional associations would see these journals. At present the only publication to list all types of courses which might be useful to various branches of the profession is the *Professional Calendar* published by the Department of Information and Library Studies at the University of Wales (Aberystwyth). Even here, there is little attempt to indicate at what level individual courses are aimed, but courses are priced and indexed by subject, organizer and location, which is very helpful.

The professional association must recognize that the range of skills needed by one-person librarians is very broad, and some of these may be better taught by organizations other than the Library Association or Aslib. Professional opinion shows that the associations should be putting their combined weight behind a concerted effort to improve further education and training, not just for one-person librarians but for the library and information services profession as a whole. They should also be encouraging employers to take the continuing education and training needs of their information staff at least as seriously as all their other staff and to be prepared to finance this training properly.

Professional Associations in the United States

Information professionals in the United States are fortunate in having the Special Libraries Association which is, amongst other things, responsible for the continuing education and training needs of special librarians, including one-person librarians. The Solo Librarians Division is one of the fastest growing units of the SLA, and is proving to be highly successful. In addition, the Special Libraries Association supports an excellent scheme of education credits awarded to course participants which works as follows: the organization has established an official Professional Development programme, adopting the standards of the Council on the Continuing Education Unit.

The Council is a nationally recognized, non-profit federation of non-credit continuing education providers devoted to improving the quality of education, training and development. The Council approves providers of continuing education who meet a stringent set of guidelines for programme administration, design and evaluation. Approved providers are eligible to award Continuing Education Units (CEUs) to programme participants. These are awarded according to the number of instructional contact hours included in an organized education programme i.e. a full-day continuing education course would have more units awarded than a half-day course, and so on. The recording of CEUs by the Special Libraries Association provides its members with a permanent, standardized record of their continuing education achievements. In addition, CEUs would certainly be a positive advantage to an individual when compiling a curriculum vitae. Unfortunately, at the time of writing, no such scheme exists in the UK.

The part that employers should play in training

Employers should first assess what they require from their library and information centres. If management does not realize what kind of services can be provided by the staff of a well-managed information centre and the enormous savings which can be made to the company by the provision of timely and accurate information, then the centre will never achieve its full potential. Employers need also to be made aware of the wide range of skills possessed by the information staff (everything from translation to online searching), and also their further training and updating needs. Induction training should always be provided for new recruits. Indeed, any training (as distinct from continuing education) should always be carried out in the firm's own time, and one-person librarians should be allowed time off to attend relevant short courses, especially now that, in the UK, an alternative method of becoming a chartered librarian places the onus on employers to provide the relevant training. For details on becoming chartered, one-person librarians in the UK should read *Routes to Associateship*, available from the Education Department of the Library Association. Employers can only benefit from the improved education standards of their employees, and should allow staff to attend continuing education programmes, perhaps by way of short periods of leave, and recognize that both work efficiency and motivation will be improved as a result.

Clearly, the message is getting across to employers and many good training practices do exist in both UK and international firms. One only has to read Sylvia Webb's report *Best Practice? Continuing Professional Development for Library/Information Staff in UK Professional Firms*[10] to see that training and continuing education of library and information services staff is alive and well in some sectors, and the situation is the same in the United States. Any organization puzzling about the training needs of its library and information services staff would be advised to read the Webb report, as it sets out very clearly some excellent examples of training schemes in various fields such as law, accountancy, architecture, banking, insurance and engineering consultancy.

Conclusion

One-person librarians wanting to find out more about training and continuing education should read not only the Williamson study but also look at Marcus Woolley's detailed observations on professional development and professional management in a one-person library.[11] The latter provides a full case study of the training process experienced by a one-person librarian early in his career, and forms part of a professional development report submitted to the Library Association for registration. Joan Williamson's study details continuing education and training problems encountered by one-person librarians, with possible and actual solutions. Anyone wishing to devise his or her own training programme should read these plus the chapter on *Training in Industrial and Commercial Libraries*, by Margery Hyde, in the *Handbook of Library Training Practice*, Volume 2.[12]

References

1   National Economic Development Council/Manpower Services Commission, *Training and Education in the Federal Republic of Germany, the United States and Japan.* NEDC/MSC, 1984.

2   Coopers and Lybrand, *A challenge to complacency: changing attitudes to training.* Coopers and Lybrand, 1986.

3   Open University Committee on Continuing Education, *Report of the Committee on Continuing Education.* Open University, Milton Keynes, UK. 1975.

4   Weingard, D.C.. 'The information hotseat: continuing education in a changing world', *Journal of Education for Librarianship*, 24, (4), 1984.

5   Association of American Library Schools, 'Policy statement on continuing library and information science education'. *Journal of Education for Librarianship*, 21, (4), 1981.

6   Slater, Margaret, 'Investment in training: a quick, qualitative conspection in the library-information field', *British Library R&D Report 6048*, BLRDD, 1991.

7   Gabarro, John J. and Kotter, John P., *Managing Your Boss*, HBR Classic NO 80104, Cambridge, MA, Harvard Business Review, 1979.

8   Williamson, Joan. 'One person libraries and information units: their education and training needs', *Library Management*, 9 (5), MCB Press, Bradford, West Yorkshire: 1988.

9   Saunders, W.L., *Towards a Unified Professional organization for Library and Information Science Services: a Personal View*, Viewpoints on LIS 3. The Library Association, London: 1989.

10   Webb, Sylvia P., Best Practice? Continuing Professional Development for Library/Information Staff in UK Professional Firms, *British Library R&D Report 6039*. Sylvia Webb, Berkhamsted, Herts: 1991.

11   Woolley, Marcus, 'The One-Person Library: Professional Development and Professional Management', *Library Management* 9, (1). MCB Press, Bradford, West Yorkshire, 1988.

12   Prytherch, Ray (ed), *Handbook of Library Training Practice*. Vol. 2. Gower Press, London: 1990.

Chapter Five

The one-person librarian: the best person for the job

Success in the one–person library does not come easy. There are, perhaps, those who see one–person librarianship as something of a sinecure, as an opportunity to get away from the 'real world' (whatever that might be). They see one–person librarianship as a career choice where they can closet themselves in a tightly structured, carefully controlled work environment. They have been misinformed. In fact, the one–person librarian is required to work harder, move faster, compete, judge, and be judged in an environment that is probably more demanding than any other situation in the library and information services profession. There is no one else to ease the burden; the one–person librarian is single–handedly responsible for the success or failure of the library, and when there is failure, there is no one else to take the blame. For the one–person librarian, accountability is the ever-present characteristic of his or her job, the one constant that is always part of the routine. The information professional who chooses to work in the one–person library must accept from the beginning that the success of the operation that is his responsibility is going to be based directly on his own personal success in the performance of his duties. This is not a bad thing. For the person who is excited by challenge in the workplace, who accepts with some enthusiasm the responsibilities of managing a tightly controlled, highly visible activity, and who has confidence in herself and her abilities to provide the services she has agreed to provide, the one–person library can be a rewarding, constantly exciting and intellectually satisfying place to work.

Confidence

In just about every walk of life, confidence in one's own abilities and professional strengths is a key to success, and it is no less necessary in the one–person library. Certainly in the business world, especially the area of small business (to which one–person librarians can relate), the success of any venture depends on the confidence of the people involved. John Nathan, an award-winning filmmaker and businessman, sent this message to the business community when he talked about confidence, and what he said could be a rallying cry for the one–person librarian as well:

I've been in the presence of some powerful and original thinkers.... From what I've seen, people like that are insulated to a remarkable degree against self–doubt, which is the source of power in many who are able to control their worlds.... They seem to have a highly articulated vision of the world they inhabit and of how they want it to be.... They have the energy to put into realization the smallest detail. It's an important empowerer; it allows you to communicate your vision to everyone around you with maximum efficiency and persuasiveness. There's a lot of energy and power in there.[1]

Indeed, empowerment is what this book is about – empowerment and vision. For in order to provide the excellence of service that the one–person librarian is hired to provide, this employee must have the vision to recognize what that service can be, and he or she must be empowered to achieve that service. The one–person librarian must be authorized to make management decisions about information, services, financial commitment, and, most important, about the library's contribution to the success of the mission of the organization providing its financial support. To achieve this power, the one–person librarian combines that vision of what the library can be with the confidence to bring it about.

Self-analysis

There is a variety of what might be called 'basic' characteristics for success in a one–person library, and first on the list is the ability to appraise oneself frankly and objectively. The demands of a one–person library are rigorous, and any employee in such a situation (or any library or information professional contemplating employment in a one–person library) must think about the following questions:

1. Why do I do this? Why do I work (or want to work) in this library?

2. Am I willing to make sacrifices to meet my goals?

3. Will my health and spirit withstand the demands?

4. Can I identify with the parent organization? Am I a team player?

5. Am I emotionally fit?

6. Can I take disappointment without putting the blame on someone else?

7. Can I communicate effectively? Can I deliver my message to others, particularly to those who are in a position to act on my message?

8. Do I have adequate support for what I am charged to do in this one–person library?

Basic characteristics

For a successful career in the one–person environment, self–motivation is obviously required. All the duties involved in managing an information activity, with the possible exception of readers' queries, are performed because the librarian knows they are to be done. Even readers' queries, which would seem to spring from the users, in an ideal setting are stimulated and influenced by the outreach efforts of the librarian. The successful one–person librarian knows how to provide her own stimulation for the work she is required to do.

Similarly, the one–person librarian must have the ability to work alone, frequently under pressure, and must be able to prioritize his tasks. He must be willing to interrupt any task to respond to a user's query, and he must be able to walk away from that task, work with the user for however long is required, and then return to the task and continue as if he had never been interrupted. It is not easy, but being able to deal with such interruptions is a primary requirement for working in a one–person library.

The librarian must have an interest in – and an understanding of – the goals of the parent organization. Discussed in detail later in this book, this one characteristic seems obvious, but there are frequent occasions in which a librarian seeking employment will accept a position, often in a one–person environment, and discover only later that he or she is not in sympathy with the goals of the organization which supports the library. Today, especially, with so much emphasis on the politically correct environment, taking a job in an organization with which one is out of tune is not only unfair to the organization, it lessens the commitment to service on the part of the librarian and, sad to say, can lead to a certain level of arrogance and disdain for those who are employing the librarian, to say nothing of the users of the library. The one–person library exists to serve the parent institution; the librarian who is not willing to be part of that effort does her institution, and herself as a practising professional, a disservice.

High standards of excellence are demanded of the one–person librarian, and the successful employee in this environment will commit himself to high standards simply because the rewards are so satisfying. At the same time, because he is the only employee performing these tasks, he is accountable for his actions and he cannot blame someone else when he is tempted to complete his work in a mediocre and routine manner. He is always expected to do his best, a criterion that on many occasions is quite daunting; and the circumstances of his employment do not permit him to do less.

Social skills are required. The ability to get along with other managers in the organization, with those who use the library or information centre, with those who do not use the library (and in their ignorance are sometimes even disdainful of the work the librarian performs), with one's supervisors and with those outside the organization with whom the librarian is required to interact, is not a matter in which the one–person librarian has a choice.

All of these people, at one time or another, will be in a position to pass judgement on the performance of the librarian. It is up to her to see that she is, at all times, prepared and willing to interact with these people in a manner consistent with the level of excellence that she has agreed to provide.

Because the one–person librarian works alone, he or she must maintain a high energy level. It seems to be the standard today to expect more and more from employees, so for that reason alone it is to the librarian's benefit to stay healthy, to get some exercise, and to come to work rested and prepared to meet the challenges of the day. For the manager in a one–person environment, the requirement is doubly emphasized, for when tasks must be postponed because one doesn't feel up to them, there is no-one else to do them. Those same tasks will be there waiting when the librarian gets to feeling better, and the added pressure of 'catching up' simply makes the tasks seem worse than they are. Staying healthy and working at a steady pace are the best antidotes to falling behind.

Other characteristics which are probably necessary for success in any library, but which are particularly valuable for the one–person librarian include good recall (not a photographic memory, but the ability to remember that a question or subject has come up before), curiosity, the ability to plan, and a certain level of responsibility about one's position and the level of service it requires. The successful one–person librarian has some skill at teaching, and good, solid communication skills, including the ability to speak and write clearly and concisely, are required. A librarian, especially a one–person information professional who is interacting daily with his users, must also be educated. Not only is he trained in the formal sense described in the previous chapter, but he is also adept in keeping up with current trends in the profession, knowing what is of interest and current to the users of the library, and in particular being aware of those trends and activities, both inside the parent organization and in the larger community outside, that affect management and the decisions that management must make about the organization and the milieu in which it operates.

Ideal qualities

In addition to these basic requirements, which every one–person library manager must bring to the workplace, there are other qualities which bring the librarian even closer to achieving that high level of excellence necessary for the successful one–person library. Although not addressing one–person librarians in particular, Shirley Echelman[2] offers good advice in a provocative essay on the similarities between managing a small library and managing a business. In her essay, Echelman provides a useful set of criteria against which the committed one–person librarian can judge himself or herself:

- Analytical intelligence. Walking a problem through your mind, step by step, examining each step as it is made, and arriving at a conclusion based on careful examination of all available possibilities.

- Self-confidence, including a belief in one's own judgement.

- Flexibility, that quality which allows one to be persuaded by fact and reason, but not too easily.

- A highly developed sense of humour. Not much elaboration is necessary on this point.

- Patience and a high frustration level. Working through a problem, be it the year's budget or the floor plan of a new library, with colleagues whose interests may differ greatly from yours, whose job it may be to keep your budget down while you are convinced it must rise can be an excruciating exercise in patience. And since the nature of the corporate experience is to balance departmental against overall goals, frustration is a frequent occurrence.[2]

Another approach to effective management in the one-person library comes from Rosabeth Moss Kanter.[3] Known in the management field for recognizing that certain people in an enterprise contribute to its success by bringing about change in the organization, Kanter identified certain characteristics in these 'change masters', as she called them. While most one-person librarians probably do not think of themselves as affecting change in their organizations, many of these characteristics can in fact lead to success in the one-person environment. For example, change masters are people who tune into their environment. These one-person librarians know what is going on in the organization in which they work, and they know what is happening beyond the immediate vicinity of the library. They take advantage of cross-disciplinary contact, and they use these contacts when they can be helpful in solving problems connected with the library and its services.

Change masters are creative, and these one-person librarians recognize that there is never only one way to solve a problem. They learn not to take things too seriously and when confronted with a problem they give themselves time to think about it as they search for a solution. They also have a clear vision: they know what the payoff from their ideas will be, and they are not afraid to express those ideas. They find themselves supported by the organization that supports the library, and they are not afraid to ask, 'What have we got to lose?'

Change masters build coalitions and create alliances, and these one-person librarians recognize the important people in the organization. They let them know what the library can do for them, and they find themselves valued very highly in the organizational structure.

Kanter's change masters work through teams. They are one-person librarians who get involved, who know what projects the organization is working on and how the library directly affects the success of those projects. They are not in a subservient role – they are part of the team that makes things happen.

Change masters persevere and persist. One–person librarians who suc-ceed don't give up. If they have a new way of doing something, or a keen idea that will bring better service to their users, they pursue it and keep pursuing it, for they have confidence that they will succeed at what they are doing.

Finally, change masters make everyone a hero. Nobody innovates alone, not even a one–person librarian working without anyone else in the library. There are those – management, other employees, users – who help the librarian achieve some of the library's goals, and when they do, they are rec-ognized for their contributions to the success of the library.

In addition to the concepts provided by Echelman and Kanter, further characteristics for success in a one–person library come from Ann W. Talcott,[4] who in 1987 participated in a special 'Presidential Task Force' of the Special Libraries Association to study the value of the information pro-fessional. In the published report, many of the qualities Talcott requires of the successful information professional relate to the characteristics identi-fied above, but there are unique approaches in her list. The one-person librarian seeking to achieve success benefits from establishing that his or her qualifications include:

- An understanding of the business and a knowledge of the company (including the corporate culture)

- An intuitive feeling of what the client is looking for without his/her artic-ulating it

- Expert knowledge of the most productive sources to pursue for the information, whether online (full–text vs. abstracts) or print

- The ability to determine the most effective packaging: summarize, high-light essence of articles, prioritize articles (e.g. 'must read', 'read if you have time', 'read if you have extra time'), prepare graphics, etc.

- The ability to communicate effectively, whether the enquirer is a scien-tist, executive or executive secretary; expert listener

- Interest in his own and his clients' work

- A strong commitment to quality service

- The ability to estimate what is possible, especially as far as delivery schedules are concerned; coupled with a willingness not to promise what can't be delivered

- The ability to concentrate total effort for a short period of time on a pro-ject, finish it on schedule whilst knowing that more information may be available post–deadline; to drop a project when it's over (again, despite knowing that more information would be available if he/she had more time to search for it)

- The ability to juggle several projects at once

- Discretion with users, with management, with other staff in the organization

The one–person librarian is a breed apart, and as far as library and organizational management is concerned, it soon becomes apparent in any discussion of skills and qualifications that special abilities are needed to manage successfully in the one–person environment. This is, of course, in direct contradiction to the common perception. Both inside the library and information services profession and in the non-professional community as well, most people seem to assume that managing a one–person library is nothing more than a simplified or pared-down version of general library or small business management. In fact the duties and responsibilities in successful one–person library management demand a level of expertise and commitment far beyond those required for general library work. Whether he chose his job in the one–person library, or simply found himself, through a combination of circumstances, working in this milieu, the successful one–person librarian recognizes that his calling is one that requires his best talents and his best effort. He welcomes the challenge.

References

1 'Coming of age', *Inc.*, 11, 4, April, 1989, 39.

2 Echelman, Shirley. 'Libraries are businesses, too!' *Special Libraries*, 65, 413, (October/November) 1974.

3 Kanter, Rosabeth Moss. *The Change Masters*. Touchstone (S&S), New York, 1985.

4 Talcott, Ann W., 'A Case Study in Adding Intellectual Value: The Executive Information Service', The President's Task Force on the Value of the Information Professional Final Report Preliminary Study. Washington DC,: Special Libraries Association, 1987.

Chapter Six

The role of the one-person library

From time to time in the library and information services profession, there is considerable disagreement about allegiance. Is a librarian an independent practitioner? As a member of a group which calls itself a 'profession' and whose role is to serve as a consultant and scholar (as described by Robert Hauptman [1]), does this person not stand above the crowd, providing services based on altruism, wisdom and independence? Or is this employee simply one of several employees, merely there to serve as a functionary and, in the case of the librarian, to provide information and materials requested by other 'knowledge workers' (as defined by Peter Drucker back in 1966 [2]) who themselves know what they need to do their work and merely require a librarian to obtain it for them? Obviously neither of these extremes properly represents the role of the librarian, but most members of the profession find themselves grappling with these questions at some point in their careers. It is a quandary for many librarians and, as we shall see, there have been satisfactory resolutions for some. For others the picture is not clear, and they continue to find themselves torn between allegiance to the organization which employs them (even, for some public librarians, to the community or other local authority which provides financial support for the library) and the profession they entered so that they could, indeed, contribute significantly to others' quests for information and knowledge.

The one–person librarian is luckier than most, for by working alone to provide the services that support the organization employing her, she is in a position to know more about what is going on, what the needs of the organization and its employees are, and how she, in her unique capacity, can be part of the organizational effort.

The mission of the parent organization.

The manager of a one–person library cannot do his job if he does not clearly understand the mission of the organization that employs him. All too often the lines become blurred and the one-person library manager finds himself pulled in a variety of directions, trying to please many different users, each with a separate agenda for the organization. A manufacturing plant, for example, will certainly have as part of its mission the development and creation of whatever product is manufactured there. The plant might also be the only major employer in a large rural area, where social services are limited, and in order to be of service to the community, the plant might take on the responsibility of providing education counselling for young people, or health services for the families of employees, or financial services in the form of a credit union established to serve the employees and others in the community. What, then, is the mission of the organization, and to what extent is the research facility in the plant – its library – expected to support that mission?

Similarly, a museum with an exceptional collection and a highly educated curatorial staff might enter into the community education field, offering courses in cooperation with a nearby university's art department, and members of the community discover that an important resource – the museum's library which had been created for the support of curatorial research – is now available to support their educational endeavors. What is the mission of the museum, and, again, what role is the library to play in the support of that mission?

Such are the questions one–person library managers often find themselves asking, and the answers can be found in the organizational mission statements, as published or otherwise disseminated. A mission statement primarily lays out the organization's mission. It describes the fundamental reasons why the organization exists, establishes the scope of the work of the organization, and describes, usually in very general terms, how the organization operates.

Most of us assume that all organizations have mission statements and that, for the one–person librarian who is determined to establish the role of the library in the organization, all that is needed is a quick look at the organizational statement. This is not always so easy. For the one–person library operating as a department of a major corporation or university, or even a branch of a public library system, there will probably be a statement of mission available. Many other one–person librarians, however, find themselves unable to determine an organizational mission, as they are employed by very small companies – a two– or three–partner law firm, for example, or an architectural firm with a total staff of only 16 employees – and management has simply never got around to putting together a formal mission statement. On the other hand, in the non–profit or not–for–profit sector – small historical societies, small hospitals, philanthropical organizations and the like – mission statements are easier to come by, for most of these organizations are required by law to file mission statements with appropriate governmental bodies, if they are to benefit from contributions deductible from the donors' taxes. Even in these environments, however, the actual services provided by the organization, and expected of the one–person library, are often at odds with what is recorded, simply because the organization, in its attempts to serve as broad a population base as possible, permits itself to offer services beyond the scope of its designated mission.

In order to determine the mission of the organization, the one–person librarian must first stop and give himself time to 'have a good think' about the parent organization and its work. That in itself may provide enough information to enable him to establish connections within the organization, so that he can relate his work to theirs. If he needs more specific information, he can look for materials published about the organization (annual reports, reports to partners and stockholders, house organs, etc.), or seek out memoranda and mission statements from other employees. If he is seriously interested in finding answers he cannot find elsewhere, he might ask for conversations with senior management, in order to fill in some philosophical background about the organization, particularly if there is no published mission statement. For he will very quickly discover that having a clear understanding of the mission of the organization is vital to his ability to provide the level of service he has committed himself to.

The lines of authority

An important step in establishing the role of the library in the parent organization is to determine the lines of authority. Again, in the very small organization, the lines will be clearly drawn from day one, for the new employee will meet her immediate supervisor, discover how strictly or loosely the lines of authority are observed, and proceed to participate in the work of the organization very quickly.

In some cases, the supervising authority may not be on the same premises as the library (for example, the very small branch of a large public library system, a departmental library located across the campus from the main college library, or a resource centre for a scientific institute whoose main headquarters are located elsewhere). In such cases, the first consideration is for the one–person librarian to seek out and understand clearly who it is that he or she reports to. This may seem obvious, but there are many variations and so many different types of parent organizations in which one–person libraries operate that what may seem obvious is not necessarily so. For example, in an information unit in the research and development section of a large commercial firm, one might expect the managers of the research unit to supervise the librarian. Yet the library might be part of an administrative services unit, along with the secretarial pool, the mail room and/or the personnel unit. Similarly, because staff training is part of the work of the human resources department, and because materials used in staff training are coordinated through the research library, the manager of the one–person research library might find herself reporting to the head of human resources – a not uncommon situation in some organizations. In another situation, fairly common in the corporate world, the director of the executive library in a firm is supervised by the vice-president for public relations. There is no 'normal' reporting structure for one–person libraries; if there is any typical characteristic, it is that these libraries can be found anywhere in the organizational structure.

If the structure is unclear and the one–person librarian is not comfortable with the information she has, there are ways to find out what she needs to know. In many cases, just seeing the organizational flowchart is enough, but some delicacy and tact might be needed, depending on who will provide the information. If the parent organization is large enough to have several departments, it is likely that at some point in its history, flowcharts have been devised and one exists with the library's place on it. If the flowchart is not offered, the one–person librarian must ask to see one, since it is impossible to contribute successfully to the organization without knowing what the lines of authority are.

Working with the immediate manager or supervisor

If the role of the one–person library is to support the organization, the organization is likewise required to support the library as it provides the information services the organization must have to fulfill its mission. Managers should be encouraged to look upon the relationship with the one–person librarian as a partnership, and as the organization's representative in the partnership, the librarian's immediate supervisor or manager plays a vital role in the process. It is therefore necessary for both the librarian and his or her supervisor to recognize that, as far as information services are concerned, the two must share common expectations about the service and must cooperatively plan the programmes of the one–person library (although, as the library manager, the librarian has the professional expertise and authority for making decisions about the operation of the facility). Good communication and information sharing is a basic requirement between the one–person librarian and the supervisor, and working together they will evaluate the progress of specific programmes and goals affecting the delivery of information services.

In this partnership, neither the librarian nor the supervising manager behaves as superior or inferior, for both parties recognize that a common understanding of their goals and of why they are being pursued, and of how the one–person library will reach those goals, are all part of the working arrangement. In this context, the role of the one–person librarian as a library manager changes, and she takes on four distinct attributes, serving the organization as:

- information provider
- administrator
- entrepreneur
- public relations practitioner [3]

Each of these roles offers a different approach to the usual relationship between the librarian and the supervisor or manager, and enables the librarian to present the library in a light that demonstrates its value to the operations of the organization as a whole.

The library's mission

The obvious beginning for a discussion of the library's mission is simply to state that the library supports the organization by providing information services that enable the organization to fulfil its mission. This is very close to how special libraries define themselves, and for the purposes of looking at the one–person library's role in the organization, a consideration of the special library branch of the library and information services profession is useful.

Although the general thesis of this book is that the principles of management described are equally applicable in any type of one–person library, there are some subjects in which the concepts from a specific type of library are best applied to the one–person library environment. The role of the library in the organization is one of those subjects, for it is here that the one–person library can best be appreciated. Even in academic and public library situations, when the providing of library services is the responsibility of only one staff member, that library can be called a 'special' library because it shares certain qualities that all special libraries share. If we look at one–person library management in these terms, the role of the library in the organization becomes clearer.

Helen J. Waldron identified several of these elements that distinguish special librarianship from traditional librarianship.[4] Her list includes such things as the offering of a very specialized and personalized service, which is characterized as 'both a philosophy and a practice'. Any library small enough to be managed by one person, regardless of its connection with the organization or the community, is going to offer personalized service, simply because the librarian will get to know the users very well and be able to anticipate their information needs.

Likewise, Waldron suggests that a special library is concerned primarily with current information, which again defines most one–person libraries. While there are those organizations which provide traditional library services, the primary value of a one–person library is the provision of information, usually very quickly and requiring of the librarian an expenditure of energy which precludes her taking on any other task while she is seeking that information. It is the immediacy of the material that is called for in most one–person libraries, and the information professionals who manage these libraries long ago realized that wherever the information can be found, regardless of the medium, that is where the librarian will go for it. Hence we have one–person libraries with books, certainly, but also keeping current periodicals, technical reports and a variety of other 'hard copy' products which they use in combination with online and other electronic sources such as CD–ROM. For the one–person librarian, the faster she can get the information, the happier her users are going to be.

Certainly many one–person libraries are special libraries as defined by Wilfred Ashworth in *Special Librarianship*.[5] He described a special library as one which is established 'to obtain and exploit specialized information for the private advantage of the organization which provides its financial support'. Sylvia Webb, in her book on setting up an information service, suggests that such libraries result from 'the realization that the organization needs information regularly, and is aware that having a central point of reference for information enquiries is likely to be more efficient and effective than the "shot in the dark" approach'.[6] In the United States, Elizabeth Ferguson and Emily R. Mobley established a standard definition of the library and the librarian:

> A special library is characteristically a unit or department of an organization primarily devoted to other than library or educational purposes. A special librarian is first an employee, a staff member of the parent organization, and second a librarian. 'Special' really means library service specialized or geared to the interests of the organization and to the information needs of its personnel.[7]

Grieg Aspnes, in a classic essay on the philosophy of special librarianship,[8] makes reference to another difference between special and traditional library work: 'The special librarian's methods may be less formal, more experimental, with a greater tendency to use shortcuts or adopt novel techniques', and he adds one more important element to the special librarian's role: responsibility for providing a total information service. It is our contention that these characteristics describe the one–person library, regardless of setting, as well as those libraries which might be thought of as specifically 'special'.

Job description

In order for the one–person librarian to play an effective role in meeting the organization's information needs, her job description must reflect the actual duties she is called upon to perform. While there are many samples of job descriptions, a criteria–based performance evaluation developed for hospital library managers and published in *Special Libraries* (and reprinted in *The One–Person Library* newsletter) is an excellent example for the one–person librarian.[9] The description begins with a statement of the educational qualifications for the position ('The library manager has a master's degree in library science from an accredited school of library science') as well as a note of experience and specific continuing education coursework requirements. The description also spells out in specific terms the organizational reporting structure and lists the responsibilities of the position. It is worth reprinting here:

Knowledge

1. Demonstrates a sound knowledge base related to management principles.

2. Demonstrates expertise in the delivery of library services as related to the library.

Planning/organization

3. Develops, achieves and evaluates departmental goals.

4. Identifies, anticipates and prepares for future library needs.

5. Directs departmental operations in a planned systematic manner.

Budget planning/control

6. Forecasts short- and long- term fiscal needs and revenue sources of the library in concert with overall hospital goals.

7. Manages financial resources of the department in a cost-effective manner.

Human relations

8. Demonstrates open and direct communication skills.

9. Promotes and maintains effective intra- and interdepartmental working relationships.

10. Fosters positive community relations.

Problem solving/conflict resolution

11. Demonstrates ability in problem solving and decision making.

12. Provides leadership in effective resolution of potential or actual conflicts within and outside the department.

Emergency situations

13. Maintains departmental operations during crisis and emergency situations.

Safety/environment

14. Directs the maintenance of the work environment.

15. Identifies problems related to safety, sanitation and maintenance of the environment, and directs the resolution of any problems.

Legal issues

16. Demonstrates knowledge of legal issues related to departmental operations.

17. Identifies areas pertinent to risk management and incident prevention.

Standards/quality

18. Coordinates departmental standards and quality assurance activities.

Leadership

19. Provides organization–wide leadership in areas of expertise.

20. Cooperates and contributes to attainment of organizational goals and objectives.

21. Represents the organization in community events and/or professional activities.

Professional development

22. Demonstrates self-directed learning in professional continuing education.

Other

23. Performs other duties as necessary or as assigned.

The role of the one–person librarian

Every organization must have information to survive – not for nothing do Japanese companies hire 'information–gathering' experts. It must be the right information at the right time, and the information must be good and opportune. Information of one sort or another is needed every day, several times a day, by many different people for different reasons. The one–person librarian acts as a catalyst or facilitator with this information, the 'kingpin' (in the old–fashioned figurative sense: the most important person in a group) between departments of an organization. People in the organization know about their own responsibilities, but they do not know much about the areas which are the responsibility of others. Added to this, they know little about the published and online sources from which information can be obtained; or what they do know is limited to their particular field of expertise. They are not trained in finding information – their job is to use it after it has been found for them, and the employee who finds it is the one–person librarian.

In fulfilling this function as information catalyst, the one-person librarian effectively becomes an in-house consultant (or as some American firms now call their librarians, 'information counselor'[10]), the acknowledged expert in the organization's information management operations. As such, she pulls together the information needed by the various departments, enabling them to work better with one another – a value which must usually be pointed out to management.

The role of the one–person library as seen by senior executives in the corporate world was lucidly described in a report of a study conducted in 1990. The findings are relevant to all one–person libraries, regardless of type, for they show how the modern information worker is perceived by those at senior management levels. The summary report states that the typical library is a centralized unit designed to identify, acquire and disseminate information. Users place the highest value on the service of database searching, with the most frequent user groups being in marketing/sales and in technical departments. An important conclusion was that there is little consensus on which library services bring the most value to the firm, and there was little agreement on how to evaluate the library's impact on the organization.[11]

Based on this summary and their analysis of the data, the researchers (James Matarazzo, Laurence Prusak and Michael R. Gauthier) concluded that:

* Librarians evaluate their performance based on standardized library methodologies. Their managers use far different, and often subjective, evaluation criteria.

* There is little management consensus on how the library adds specific value to the firm's performance, or how value should be measured.

* Librarians have little say on the firm's information policies and mission.

* Growing end–user usage of database systems and other information technologies will have a serious impact on business operations as well as on the role of the library within the firm. Will the librarian perform as purchasing agent, gatekeeper, network manager, internal trainer, information specialist, or chief information officer? Librarians and their managers have done very little planning on this critical issue.

* There is still a strong reservoir of goodwill and affection for the library and librarians, often based on an intuitive 'feel' that the service is valuable and worthy of continued support. ...it is questionable whether libraries can grow based on these forms of approval.[12]

Organizational placement

Wilfred Ashworth suggests that in order to perform most effectively, the librarian should be part of the organization's management structure:

> ...the ideal situation is for the head of the library service to have managerial status through which he will derive the necessary knowledge (directly as part of the managerial team) of the continually changing aims of the organization, of the potential for future growth and of the constraints under which the organization has to operate. This will enable him to assess which information can be profitably used, and also that which is unlikely, from lack of proper resources, to be exploitable. The nature of his work subjects him to a constant flow of new information from outside, and this makes him one of the best–informed people on the staff about external developments in the organization's field of

interest. As a manager, he would be able to use this information more directly in policy making, and not merely be a passer–on of information who might distort or fail to use it. The fewer steps there are in the transfer of information the better, as there is always the risk of distortion or inaction. The librarian's task is to use the knowledge that he acquires from his position to enable his unit to tap the most appropriate sources of information and select that part which has the highest potential for exploitation.[5]

Whether she is placed as a manager in the organization or performs her duties at another level in the managerial structure, the one–person library has specific responsibilities. While there are variations in specific situations, a useful list was prepared by Ellis Mount [12] and includes the following:

- relating to top management
- planning
- budgeting
- organizing
- marketing
- evaluating operations
- using management tools

Echelman, on the other hand, narrows the responsibilities to two, but like Koch with her first two responsibilities, lists management strengths before library skills. The distinction is important, for in the one–person library, the value of the librarian is quite often as much for his management and organizational expertise as it is for his informational skills, and the fact that these criteria are recognized has much to do with how the one–person librarian is perceived in his organization. Echelman writes that the librarian's responsibilities are:

> ...to establish and maintain liaison with other department and division managers, to ascertain needs and evaluate trends, and to direct the work of the library so that it meets current needs and is prepared for changes in direction before they occur, and ...to manage the operations of the library.[13]

For the one–person librarian who confidently carries out these responsibilities, the satisfactions of managing an effective and responsive information organization become part of her daily work, and her role is seen by managers, users and other employees, as vital to the success of the organization.

References

1 Hauptman, Robert. *Ethical Challenges in Librarianship,* Oryx Press, Phoenix, AZ, 1988, p. 14.

2 Drucker, Peter F. *The Effective Executive*. Harper and Row, New York, 1966. p. 3

3 St. Clair, Guy, 'Library management: what does it mean to you?' *Library Management Quarterly*, 9, (4), Spring, 1986.

4 Waldron, Helen J., 'The business of running a special library', *Special Libraries,* 62, February 1971, p. 63.

5 Ashworth, Wilfred, *Special Librarianship*, Clive Bingley, London, 1979, p. 6.

6 Webb, Sylvia P., *Creating an Information Service*. Aslib, London, 1983, p.1.

7 Ferguson, Elizabeth and Mobley, Emily R., *Special Libraries at Work*, Library Professional Publications, Hamden, Connecticut, an imprint of the Shoe String Press, 1984, p.4.

8 Aspnes, Grieg, 'A philosophy of special librarianship', in: E. Jackson, (ed.), *Special Librarianship: A New Reader*. The Scarecrow Press, Metuchen, New Jersey and London, 1980, p. 1.

9 Koch, Heidi C., 'Criteria–based performance evaluations for hospital managers', *Special Libraries*, 80, (4), Fall 1989, p. 272.

10 Esrey, William, *'Improving Productivity'*, Keynote Address at the White House Conference on Library and Information Services, Washington, DC, July 19, 1991.

11 Matarazzo, James, Prusak, Laurence, Gauthier, Michael R., *Valuing Corporate Libraries: A Survey of Senior Managers*. Washington DC, Special Libraries Association, 1990, p. 1.

14 Mount, Ellis, *Special Libraries and Information Centres: An Introductory Text*. Washington DC, Special Libraries Association, 1991, pp. 31–32.

15 Echelman, Shirley. 'Libraries are businesses, too!' *Special Libraries*, 65, Oct/Nov 1974, pp 409–410.

Chapter Seven

Advocacy for the one-person library

'You are as you are perceived.' For many years this cryptic phrase has been heard throughout the library and information services profession, as practitioners have come to recognize that many of the problems in the workplace could be alleviated if the profession could change others' perceptions. Yet dealing with the concept can be a threatening experience, for many in the profession, including many one–person librarians, find the idea of 'image-building' to be of little interest. More important, since many people think of image as dealing primarily with dress, body language and concerns with style and fashion, thinking about image seems somewhat undignified for practitioners in a profession connected with education and learning as is the library and information services profession.

By the mid 1980s, it had became apparent that librarians, like every other group in society, were concerned about how they are perceived by those outside the profession. Building a positive image became a strong motivation for many, and the efforts of library managers such as Kaycee Hale, Executive Director of the Resource and Research Centre at the Fashion Institute of Design and Merchandizing in Los Angeles, had much to do with redefining the concept of 'image' for the librarian.[1] Through her seminars, writings and personal appearances before library and information professionals, Hale took the idea of 'positive image' beyond a concern with fashion and redefined the issue by incorporating five useful challenges to librarians:

* Change your mind set
* Take risks
* Project a stronger image
* Enjoy being noticed
* Build personal power

At the same time that Hale and others were prescribing a positive image for librarians, others in the profession were realizing that in order to succeed in providing the services they were expected to provide, a long list of problems would have to be overcome. These had primarily to do with the placement of the library in the parent organization, with one–person librarians being particularly vulnerable to problems in this area.

As discussed in the precious chapter, one–person libraries have a proper place in the organizational structure, and the librarians themselves know what it is – that to do their best work, they should be performing a managerial role. Yet many of those who supervise librarians have different ideas. As White has pointed out (despite the fact that many librarians don't want to hear these things), 'Libraries, in the common perception, are defined by clerical functions and there is enough reality to validate the generalization'.[2] Managers and supervisors who employ librarians have their own ideas about what libraries are and what librarians do. As organizational administrators, whose first loyalty must be to the organization as a whole, they are obliged to consider the one–person library as no more (but hopefully no less) than any other organizational unit.

This state of affairs in many organizations is often reflected in a lack of general support for what the one–person library contributes to the organization, in a lack of funding for appropriate library services, in the place of the librarian in the management hierarchy and, as indicated above, in the lack of a management role for the one–person librarian. Many in the profession believe that these problems can be resolved by changing the 'common perception' about libraries and librarians. The one–person librarian is, indeed, challenged to change the image.

Preconceptions are not changed overnight, however, and before librarians can go about tackling the problems of image enhancement, they must understand the milieu in which they operate. They must give some attention to why non-professionals have the image of librarians that they have. To do so, one–person librarians must understand the role that organizational loyalty and corporate culture play in their professional lives.

Loyalty

The basic nature of organizational loyalty is defined in terms of 'steadfast allegiance',[3] yet in terms of the one–person librarian and the services she provides for the organization, a loyal relationship must be built up in both directions between the librarian and others in the organization. Senior management, library users and other staff must all accept that the library exists for the benefit of the organization and the successful achievement of the organizational mission, and the librarian herself must subscribe to this commitment. Such acceptance serves to strengthen loyalty in both directions, for the benefit of both the library and the organization.

In terms of organizational loyalty, Shea has identified three key concepts which play an important role in determining the success of the relationship between the one–person librarian and the people with whom he interacts in the organization:[3]

1. Loyalty in either direction is unlikely to be absolute; indeed, the prospect is virtually impossible.

2. Some loyalties fade and therefore need to be frequently renewed, nurtured, and strengthened if they are to last.

3. Both the individual and the organization need to decide how much loyalty is appropriate, and this implies an ongoing, open, honest dialogue if neither side is to be deceived. It also requires thoughtful commitment and appropriate notice to the other party if anything affecting their loyalty 'pact' changes.

The question for the one–person librarian thus becomes one of determining the basic organizational attitude toward loyalty: is the organization one that values loyalty, and is it worthwhile for the one–person librarian to seek this two–way loyalty with others in the organization? Is loyalty rewarded in other departments in the organization? In the organization as a whole? In fact does it make any difference whether or not an employee does a good job? Finally, in terms of what the one–person library is trying to offer in the way of information services, what is the level of commitment, excellence and accountability in other 'staff' or 'management support' departments that are roughly analogous to the library in the roles they play in the organization?

Corporate culture

It was Marlene Vogelsang who identified corporate culture as an important force in the success (or failure) of a library:

> Understanding the role and influence of corporate culture can be a valuable technique in the management of a library or information centre. The prevailing culture is a reflection of the parent organization that has an impact both directly and indirectly on all departments or division.[4]

The best definition of corporate culture comes from Silverzweig and Allen: 'a set of expected behaviors that are generally supported within the group ... unwritten "rules" that have an immense impact on behavior ... (and) which affect every aspect of organizational functioning'.[5] In these terms, it is not difficult to see that corporate culture as it affects the one–person library has many ramifications, especially when we observe that other experts in the field have discovered that in organizations which are successful in achieving their organizational mission, 'shared values' (yet another way of defining corporate culture) are emphasized throughout the organization. Management success is determined by their ability to recognize and work within the corporate culture.[6] It could also be argued that the success of the one–person librarian in the organization can likewise be built on his or her talents in reading the corporate culture about information services and what is expected of the library and the librarian.

The value of the librarian

As we move through an understanding of the role of organizational loyalty and corporate culture in determining the success of the one–person library, it becomes clear that the services, the mission and the management of the library are intractably bound up with the perceived value of the librarian. It is, in fact, the perception of the librarian which determines the place of the library in the organization. That perception, like much else in our society, is based on the value of the services emanating from the one–person library in the person of the librarian who provides them.

In many organizations the one–person library is undervalued, despite the efforts of the librarian to provide the best services she can, given the limited resources and managerial support she receives. Yet she will not be given the resources and support she needs until she is able to prove her value to her management, and before she can do that, she needs to understand why she and the library's services are perceived as they are.

There are specific reasons why librarians are undervalued, and these were identified by a special study group in 1987.[7] The President's Task Force on the Value of the Information Professional, appointed by Frank Spaulding, the President of the Special Libraries Association, asked why librarians are undervalued, and came up with the following reasons:

- Library operations are usually lumped together under organizational overheads and suffer from the unit–cost bias. Information professionals are perceived to consume resources rather than generate revenue; their work cannot easily be apportioned and attributed to the unit cost of an organizations output.

- Traditionally, library products and services have been given away – they have no value attached. In today's organizational environment, a unit's services must be 'proved' worthwhile, and when they are not, they are judged to be of little value.

- Librarians have not been required to master the political and public relations skills needed to create and maintain a positive image of their own essentiality and importance. Other, more aggressive players often 'take over' research results which information librarians derive. Bypassing the library and claiming the output as their own, they deprive the library of due credit.

- Unlike a manufactured product or standard service, information is not measurable in any standard unit and thus cannot be easily priced; information worthless to one organization may be priceless to another.

- Information is not used up or degraded, either by intermediate level users or the ultimate decision maker.

- The one–person librarian's work – the creative activity that actually adds value to the otherwise inert material in the collection and makes it usable by and for clients – is unobservable mental work. Its invisibility adds to its general lack of appreciation and low valuation.

The task force asked how, in such a context, it is possible to justify the expenses of a library or information centre and explain to those who provide the funds the tremendous added value the professional staff contributes to the organization as a whole? In its report, the task force stated that this question had guided its study, and it is the same question which must guide the work of the one–person library manager. He must always be aware of these barriers to the value of his services, and seek steps to remove them whenever he can.

Perception

Not only must the one–person librarian be aware of how the value of the library is often under estimated, she must also deal with perceptions that have nothing to do with her or the services she provides. Most people who come into a library have a preconceived notion of what a librarian is like. For many reasons, librarians are thought of as not quite like other people, and these reasons are based on ideas out of the control or beyond the purview of the one–person librarian.

Concern with stereotype is not limited to the library and information services profession, but library practitioners seem to be inordinately concerned about how they are perceived by others. Much has been written on the subject, and several leaders in the profession have suggested that perhaps the solution to problems of stereo-type must come from within the profession. White, for one, has suggested that the value of the information professional (as described above) is sometimes diminished because the librarians themselves are not taking a forceful, leadership role:

> To have any hope of convincing others, we must begin with a regard for ourselves and the importance of what we do. ... The outside world won't change our profession for us. People like librarians and libraries just fine the way they see them. The willingness of users to accept poor library service is almost limitless. ... If librarianship is to change its outside perceptions it must first change its self–perceptions ... a process of evaluation which recognizes, encourages, and promotes to library leadership those restless and dissatisfied risk–takers who espouse the values and characteristics which any self–respecting profession demands of itself.[8]

Yet the fault is not all from within, and one–person librarians attempting to deal with stereotype and perception and how it affects their work, must also reflect on their responsibilities to their employer, and, in this case, to the profession of which they are a part. Probably the best analysis of this issue is found in Pauline Wilson's excellent study *Stereotype and Status: Librarians in the United States*.[9] Wilson correctly contends that the stereotype comes about because, like all stereotypes, it is based on a truth, the simple truth that 'librarians *are* charged with the responsibility of ensuring that the library is a functioning organization, that it works and works well for those who need it. And that perhaps is not without cost; part of the cost may be reflected in stereotyping'.[9] Wilson illustrates this with a long quotation from one of the respondents to the study on stereotyping in which she was involved, and it is worth repeating here, for the one–person librarian needs to be armed if he or she is going to become engaged in the battle against the stereotype which is so prevalent in the library and information services profession:

> There is a limit to the concessions we should make to redeem our image. We can afford to let the noise level rise a bit more (if they can stand it, so can we); ... we can wear two strands of beads and let our hair down; we can ... be patient teachers to those who consider the catalog an enemy fortress; ... we can sit on the floor between the stacks with our fellow researchers and pore over materials; we can confess to being no more than fellow students, on a slightly higher level, rather than acting as an authority. We can do all that.
>
> What we can't do is to say: 'Come in you dear children and take all the current magazines, never mind who needs them after you,' or 'Here are the shears, clip all the reference books you want'. We can't overlook the rowdies who prevent others from serious study, or the spoilers who stick bubble gum in the earphones and exercise their penknives on the stacks. We must watch our doors and check one hundred good readers to detect one bad one; we must insist on IDs to know who comes through our doors and to deter the thief. We are keepers of books and other media, not for our own satisfaction, but because we owe it to the reader of the future to preserve these things in order to serve him, too.
>
> What we also cannot do is to say to our workers, 'Never mind the exact spelling or alphabetical order,' or 'Relax when you shelve, a few digits off isn't the end of the world....'[9]

What do we do about the stereotype of the librarian? Wilson provides the answer in a remarkable piece of perceptive advice – we must stop talking and writing about it:

> Not only do librarians perpetuate the stereotype by keeping every librarian aware of it through journal articles, they indoctrinate new entrants into the profession early. Master's students are permitted to do theses on the stereotype as well as various classroom exercises probing the personality of the librarian. This practice not only disseminates the stereotype and gives it an unwarranted gloss of scholarship, it ensures that these new entrants into the profession begin their careers with the stereotype firmly implanted in their consciousness.[9]

Should we take Wilson's advice? Certainly in the one–person library there is no need to talk and write about stereotypes, for the interaction the one–person librarian has with her clients is, in fact, on a highly professional basis, and the accountability of the one–person situation precludes stereo-typical judgements from those who use the services of the library and are satisfied with them. The one–person librarian accepts her responsibility, and if that requires establishing procedures and regulations that others might find restrictive, too much in the 'librarian' mode, the one–person library manager has only to remind them that her work requires her to act respon-sibly. On the other hand, there will be times when (remembering Grieg Aspnes' observation noted earlier), because of the special circumstances of the one–person library, she will be able to use methods that are less formal and more experimental, including shortcuts and novel techniques. So much the better, and if she is complimented because 'You don't act like a librari-an', she simply smiles to herself, invoking Echelman's call for a sense of humour and ascribing the remark (just as she does when people accuse her of being 'too much like a librarian') to ignorance on the part of people who don't know what her job is.

Advocacy defined

Advocacy for the one–person library might be thought of as a process in which those who are in a position to affect the delivery of library services, whether as users, management or interested observers, are targeted as sup-porters for the library. With or without their active compliance, they are put in a position to recognize, evaluate and enhance the value of the library within the organization which supports it.

Advocates must be sought out. They do not automatically turn up in the library offering their help, but when they are chosen and determine that the one–person library is a part of the organization they want to support, their loyalty to the library and their interest in its well-being are assets which the manager of the one–person library will find he cannot do without.

Some librarians at this point question why the advocate for a library must be someone from outside; Why can't the one–person librarian herself be the library's best advocate? The easy answer is that she can, but not soon, and not totally by herself, for despite the excellence of her services and her dedi-cated commitment, she is nevertheless still perceived as the librarian described above, with the same misperceptions about her work and her role, and the same lack of understanding about the value of library work in general that all information workers must contend with. While she is prov-ing herself, the advocates for the one–person library are doing the same, and using their positions and authority within the organization to strength-en her role.

In the advocacy process, the first step for the one–person librarian is to understand the organization, to know intimately how it works. Helen J. Waldron has recognized that an organization can be very confusing, if not 'downright meaningless', to one not familiar with it. Each organization can be as different from other organizations as each special library can be from one another, so Waldron offers three suggestions for getting to know the organization:

- Get a clear picture of the organization's structure so that the librarian and the library can identify with its main objectives.

- Acquire a thorough understanding of the company policies within which the library will be operating – the quickest way to perdition is to attempt to operate in conflict with those general policies.

- Begin the establishment of harmonious relations with users, with peers in the organization, and with management strata above and below.[14]

Other perceptive advice comes from Elizabeth Orna, who in 1978 recognized that to build an effective strategy for information service in the organization, the one–person librarian must know the organization itself:

Although the aim is a productive interaction between the service and its users, it would be a deception to think the way to it lay through concentration on human relations, 'interactive skills', 'sensitivity', and the like. Good personal and professional relationships between information workers and their colleagues elsewhere in the organization are a necessary but not sufficient condition for ensuring effective information use. They cannot be purposeful unless they are backed by a strategy which derives from a thorough knowledge of the organization. Knowing the organization provides a frame of reference against which the various options open to the service, the allocation of resources, the priorities of individual demands, and ways into contacts with users can be evaluated and decisions taken.[11]

Orna then lists what the one–person librarian must know about the parent organization:

- organizational structure

- how power is distributed in the organization

- the way information flows through the organization

- the organization's purposes and aims

Why does a 'thorough knowledge of the organization' matter? Orna replies: 'It can help us to judge both the constraints and the opportunities which the information service has – and among the opportunities, whatever the form of the organization, is that of becoming skilled in making the organization work for us, and learning to play it as a responsive instrument.' [11]

As the one–person librarian learns the organization, he learns too the value of information to that organization – what the work he is doing means to the organization as a corporate entity. John Kok has stated that no single factor has greater influence on the library manager than the organization's attitude toward information,[12] so it is up to the librarian to determine what this attitude is – to carry out an 'attitude' audit, so to speak – in order to determine how he can use it to plan and deliver the information services he has been hired to provide.

Using management

Thus the one–person librarian learns which people have the potential to be advocates for the library. He starts with management, recognizing what David Drake pointed out to all librarians who have to report to people who are not part of the library and information services profession: 'The key to increased appreciation for library services is in the attitude of our non–librarian supervisors'.[13]

There are certain management qualities that indicate that the one–person librarian's supervisor has a supportive attitude toward the library, and several of these were identified by Meryl Swanigan in a discussion about excellence in library services. These included being open to new ideas, being supportive, chiding the mistakes of the librarian but never using them negatively, giving the librarian freedom to run her own shop, giving her few but specific parameters in which to work, and trusting the librarian.[14]

At the same time, the one–person librarian has certain obligations to management, and William S. O'Donnell lists ten objectives that management expects from the library, and which the librarian must be willing to achieve if he or she expects management to support her work:

1. A clear understanding by the librarian of the library's role in the organization's operation

2. A thorough knowledge of the industry or subject specialty of the organization

3. A detailed knowledge of the organization itself

4. Forceful insistence on adequate library tools

5. Adequate professional qualifications

6. Administrative competence

7. Skill in keeping management informed

8. A knack for clarifying users' needs

9. Empathy with users' needs

10. A sense of participation[15]

Charles Bauer, in a provocative essay entitled 'Managing Management', offers a variety of steps for ensuring that management recognize the role of the library, and his conclusion, in which he charges the library manager to seek 'management acknowledgement' (certainly a key element in our quest for advocacy) is worth reprinting here:

> Managing management is an earned privilege. It means continuous, arduous work, effective planning, proper supervision, productivity, coordination of efforts, salesmanship, and reputation for having good sense and a reliably concerned professional attitude. To become a part of management, however, take the initiative and learn how to work with management. What is earned in that role is top management's acknowledgement. Once that is attained, it is not too hard for a manager to ask top management for special needs and even some favors.[16]

There are specific steps the one–person librarian can take to increase management interest in the library and, in the process, turn supervisors into advocates for the library. Some of these suggestions are basic, but they are worth mentioning simply because the librarian often has little time or energy for thinking about these techniques. Published first in *The One–Person Library: A Newsletter for Librarians and Management*[17], these ideas are worth thinking about:

- *Establish personal contacts:* there are times when it is to the librarian's advantage to know something about a supervisor's personal interests, what some of her own professional concerns are, and similar traits which can be acted upon for maintaining better working relations. Example: Make it your business to know what particular subjects are of interest to your supervisor and regularly route materials on those subjects to her, without waiting to be asked.

- *Communicate easily:* set up routines so that you and your supervisors can talk about what's going on in the library, so that you feel comfortable about bringing up subjects that may or may not be of particular interest to them, but which for the good of the organization should be discussed openly and frankly. Example: A particularly bothersome user frequently seems to be just on the verge of making trouble – mention it casually from time to time, so that if an explosion does come, your supervisor won't be surprised and put you on the spot.

- *Know when to pull back:* there are times when, even in the most supportive of situations, your manager might have had just about enough from you. Even if the library or information service is his favourite part of the operation, it is nevertheless, only one of several areas of responsibility for him. If you are always coming to him for support, he might withhold it just to close the discussion. Example: You've been asked to draw up the specs for a new wordprocessing system for the library. Although you know what you need, you daily ask him his opinion about this feature or that special service. If you figure it out for yourself and present him with a plan, he is more likely to approve the package and support your request for it.

- *Don't create trouble unnecessarily:* you know you are there to run the library, and so does your manager. If you go to her for advice in every situation, not only are you putting your professionalism on the line, you are running the risk of making her think you aren't a good manager yourself. Save the trips to her office for major problems that you don't feel competent or skilled enough to solve. Example: A user is complaining that the library does not offer a particular service, but that service is beyond the resources and scope of the library. Take it upon yourself to explain in reasonable terms why the service is not offered. If it's not necessary to go to management, don't.

- *Stroke:* This might seem like a contradiction to the above, but it's really part of the need to maintain good relations in the workplace. Be courteous to your manager, show some respect (and even, occasionally, deference) to his position, and don't worry so much about everybody being equal, especially in the presence of others. We are not talking about mindless subservience here, for that does not belong in a professional situation, but if your demeanour always conveys a certain courteous regard for him and what he does for the organization, he is going to feel more comfortable around you. Example: Your manager walks in one morning with a visitor. You're very busy, and the visit is unexpected. Allow yourself to be interrupted, walk over and greet them, and make them feel welcome.

As an addendum to the concept of 'stroking' (and perhaps to the 'personal contact' idea as well), we should look at the role our services play in terms of how we might generate enthusiasm and interest in some of the techniques we use for information work. We might think about exploiting management interest in some of the new things that he or she, as a manager in the 1990s, must be concerned with. Andrew Berner wrote about this in 1989, suggesting that technology might be the next place for eliciting management interest in the one–person library. Berner had read that the manager of the future will need specialized knowledge directly applicable to selected tasks, and that this knowledge will be combined with hands–on familiarity with advanced information techniques. Berner goes further, demonstrating to management that the library is the logical organizational locus for developing a working knowledge of technology, and he offers four approaches for the one–person librarian to utilize in her efforts:

1. Talk to managers on a one–to–one basis. Let them know that you are available to provide this needed information to them.

2. Send memos to those you think would benefit from an increased knowledge of information technology, and explain to them just how they will benefit and how you can help. Include as many 'higher ups' as you can. In fact, go all the way to the top if you think you can.

3. If you publish a newsletter, or if your organization has a house organ, include an article on the benefits of technology and the library's role in helping managers secure that understanding. Do not simply distribute other people's thoughts on the subject. Be sure that you explain to managers how the library can help them to gain this vital knowledge.

4. If you are sufficiently knowledgeable in the area, hold seminars for managers on the subject of information technology. If you don't feel confident enough to do so, check the professional literature to find out when seminars are being offered, and be sure to announce them to management.[18]

There are, then, opportunities for the one–person librarian to work with management to interest them in the library and its services. A certain assertiveness is required, of course, and there will be those executives who will not react to the overtures of the one–person librarian. Most people, however, are flattered with attention, and if the librarian is willing to make the effort, the rewards to the one–person library, in terms of support, managerial interest and increased resources to do the job, will make the effort worthwhile.

The library committee or board

One of the primary differences between libraries in the United States and the United Kingdom, especially one–person libraries, is the use of library boards and committees. Small libraries in the United States, even in the corporate, scientific and technical worlds, frequently have a formal or informal group of users who serve as a library committee. This is not often the case in the United Kingdom.

For those one–person libraries which use a library committee or board, or for the library considering organizing one, the first requirement is that the one–person librarian understands clearly the duties, responsibilities and authority of the library board or committee in relation to the librarian and management. If possible, at the time of employment the librarian should be given written statement describing the committee's role. If it is not offered it should be requested; a written policy is not only useful for the protection of the person managing the library, but clarifies for each member of the board or committee what he or she is expected to do. This is not to suggest that an employment relationship should begin in a atmosphere of distrust, but simply to recognize that while management personnel and the library staff have accepted their positions and responsibilities as permanent, most of those who sit on boards and committees are appointed for a finite, and frequently clearly defined, period of time. Thus the committee's level of commitment can be expected to change as its membership changes, but the librarian and managerial staff will continue on a longer–term basis. To have a clearly stated and simple document outlining the obligations and responsibilities of the committee or board will, in the long run, make the librarian's organizational tasks considerably easier.

What is the role of the library board or committee? 'The principal purpose of the committee is to advise, support and guide the library director and to serve as a linkage among the users, the library, and the management', writes Jane Katayama.[19] White, too, recommends that the committee's role be advisory. It should not make policy decisions or establish priorities for the library, as 'this would be inappropriate and threatening to the librarian's management authority.'[25]

The board or committee does not (and should not) involve itself in the day–to–day operations of the library, and its public role in all cases should be one of support for the librarian and the work he is doing. Such a role might seem unobjectionable, but the temptation of power, however limited, can be irresistible to the layman who has been appointed to a committee or board, and there will be times when the librarian must educate members in their understanding of their obligations and limitations.

As long as the role played by the board or committee is advisory, and limited to that, it can be a very useful adjunct to the one–person library and its programmes. White suggests that the committee be chaired by the librarian, and that it include a broad range of individuals who 'are sensitive to or can be educated to the need for a high level of information service'.[20] White also provides a handy checklist for the committee's three roles:

- Once the committee is informed about what the library or information centre is doing and why certain policies have been promulgated, its members can pass on the information to their groups.

- The committee members can tell you what user groups need and want and what new priorities and directions are taking shape. If the library is going to provide anticipatory services it obviously needs early information, and this is an excellent way to get it.

- The committee can provide a broad and united front in communicating to higher authority what the library's needs are.

In some organizations, the one–person librarian is in the unique position of being able to determine much of what comes before the committee. It is good to bear in mind that members of the committee or board are usually not professional librarians. While they might take their positions very seriously, they are not qualified to make professional library management decisions. Frequently they have accepted the appointment as an honour or recognition and do not expect to take their work very seriously. In this case, two practical considerations are worth remembering: first, the one–person librarian should not forget that the members of the committee 'come there to play'. They are not earning their living at the library and the funds they are expending are not, in most cases, their own money. All they are obliged to give is time, which they do very generously; we must remember that they are busy and successful people or they would not have been selected for the board or committee in the first place. Many of these people do take their work very seriously and contribute a great deal to the successful operation of the library. Nevertheless, in the final analysis on any question of procedure or policy, their jobs are not on the line (as the librarian's might be). The library board and committee should be considered with this thought in mind.

A second consideration for the one–person librarian is that the board or committee will always want to look good, so it should be part of the librarian's political awareness to try to further that aim. When any member of the committee is called upon to explain some failure or lapse of service, the tendency is almost invariably to seek to place the blame elsewhere. For example, a particular user may not be satisfied with an answer to a reference question and will write a letter of complaint to the committee. To counteract such criticism it is wise to seek support in advance, which simply means that the librarian, whenever he has the opportunity, should do whatever can be done to make the board or committee look good. This does not necessarily mean that the librarian fawns over committee members or gives them special service or treatment denied to other users of the library, but only that the committee is made to know that its opinion is valued and respected. Thus, in the day-to-day operations of the library, the one–person librarian does what he can to see that the board or committee is given appropriate credit and appreciation. Such recognition may be as simple as using the phrase 'on behalf of the library committee' in acknowledging a gift to the library, or it might be just saying to someone who compliments the librarian on a good reference response that the compliment will be passed on to the library committee. The point is that the librarian and the committee support one another and are not shy about saying so in public.

The relationship between the librarian and the board of a one–person public library is very different from the private and semi–private situations many other one–person librarians work in, primarily because the legal structure of a public library involves a governing agency. This relationship has been clearly described by Dorothy Sinclair, who points out that the interest of the users and the board is one of the distinguishing characteristics of work in small libraries.[21] Similarly, other sources describe the relationship between library committees and boards for the one–person librarian who runs a school library, and since school libraries are more a part of the education profession than the library and information services profession, the librarian who is responsible for managing a school library single–handedly is referred to those sources.

It is not difficult to conclude that the librarian who supports his committee, who listens with respect when board members make suggestions, and who goes to the committee for advice and reassurance, will have established a relationship that will be very useful to him. Such activities simply recognize that these relationships are human, and as such are subject to the same sort of reactions as other human relationships. If the one–person librarian thinks of his work with the committee as mutually respectful and supportive, and not adversarial, much can be accomplished. When the librarian is on the spot, with management or with a disappointed (or even irate) user, there is much consolation in being able to say, 'Perhaps you should speak with the chairman of the library committee'. If the librarian and the committee or board can establish early on a relationship in which they see themselves working together as partners, the support from the committee or board will be there when it is needed. 'An active, interested committee can provide the library with meaningful support, sound advice and guidance, and act as liaison between the users and management'.[19]

The committee as advocate is especially useful in situations where management or a user does not understand the limitations of the library and expects more in service than can be delivered. Most lay people think they understand the management of a library, but, as is daily made clear to most librarians, they do not. Frequently the lay person will expect that a unit called a 'library' should be able to provide him with any information he seeks. It is not uncommon for a user, not understanding the limitations of a particular subject collection, to seek information that is outside the library's scope, and to be highly disappointed when a suggestion is made that he or she would do better at another library. Just as frequently the user expects the librarian to obtain the information from the other source, which, in some organizations, is not a service the library provides (although in some libraries the librarian is indeed responsible for pursuing the search elsewhere). Such limitations can be explained by referring the user to the committee or board, which, knowing the limitations of the one–person library and the services offered, will support the librarian. Playing the advocacy role is an accepted responsibility of the library board or committee, and it is to the librarian's advantage to know that he or she can count on this group for support. In summary, we once again quote Katayama: 'The relationship among library committee members, senior management personnel, and the library staff can best be described as a synergistic one, each bringing expertise and knowledge for a common goal – that of contributing to the fulfilment of the organization's mission'.[19]

Other advocates

The one–person library has yet another group of potential advocates to exploit, and Doris Bolef identified these people: when the library must be promoted among various user groups, it is not unusual to find support among the users themselves. Bolef recognizes this, and states that:

> ...selling the library can take on several forms. Often a group of patrons forms a 'belt system' around a library. Usually highly literate and interested in libraries, having used them all their lives, these patrons provide support essential to the library's well-being. They help open the channels of communication both ways, formal and informal. They serve as

sources of invaluable information to the [library] manager about the organization and where it is going. At the same time, through them the [library] manager can spread the word about the library's programmes, especially new or changed ones. Such patrons should be continually courted and the number increased with no departmental favoritism. It goes without saying that members of this group receive a higher level of service'.[22]

Considering that she has all these groups, and the many various combinations of them, available to her, the one–person librarian has a unique opportunity, as the in-house information counsellor, to make an important contribution to the success of the organization in which she is employed. Part of her task as an information consultant is to identify and work with those people in the organization who will support the level of information services she has been hired to provide. In doing so, she is able to put questions of image to rest once and for all, for the image of the one–person librarian is based on the quality of work and the excellence of the services she brings the organization. If the quest for quality and the pursuit of excellence in these services is the framework on which the one–person library and its offerings is built, and if those whose success is supported by the library are themselves in turn encouraged to support the library, questions of image will not be a concern in the one–person library.

References

1   Hale's concepts are outlined in a pamphlet published in 1988 by the Special Libraries Association, Washington DC.

2   White, Herbert S., 'Basic competencies and the pursuit of equal opportunity, part 1', *Library Journal*, 113, (12), July, 1988, p.56-57.

3   Shea, Gordon F., *Company Loyalty: Earning It, Keeping It*, American Management Association, New York, 1987, p. 16.

4   Vogelsang, Marlene., 'The reflection of corporate culture in the library or information centre', *Library Management Quarterly*, Spring 1989, pp. 16–20.

5   Shein, Edgar., *Organizational Culture and Leadership: A Dynamic View*, Jossey–Bass, San Francisco and London, 1985.

6   Deal, Terence and Kennedy, Allan, *Corporate Cultures: The Rites and Rituals of Corporate Life*, Addison–Wesley, Boston, MA, 1982.

7   *President's Task Force on the Value of the Information Professional. Final Report. Preliminary Study.* Washington DC, Special Libraries Association, 1987.

8   White, Herbert S., *Librarians and the Awakening from innocence: a collection of papers*, GK Hall, Boston, MA, 1989, p. 170.

9   Wilson, Pauline, *Stereotype and Status: Librarians in the United States, Contributions in Librarianship and Information Science, Number 41*, Greenwood Press, Westport, Connecticut, 1932.

10   Waldron, Helen J., 'The business of running a special library', *Special Libraries*, 62, February 1971, p. 66.

11   Orna, Elizabeth, 'Should we educate our users?' *Aslib Proceedings*, 30, 4, 1978, p. 132.

12   Kok, John, 'Now that I'm in charge, what do I do?' *Special Libraries*, 71, (12), December 1980, 523–528.

13   Drake, David, 'When your boss isn't a librarian,' *American Libraries*, February 1990, pp. 152–153.

14   Swanigan, Meryl, 'Managing a special library, Part II, Excellence in library management,' *Journal of Library Management*, 6, (3) Fall 1985, p. 17.

15   O'Donnell, William S., 'The vulnerable corporate special library/information centre: minimizing the risks,' *Special Libraries* 67, April 1976, pp. 179–180.

16   Bauer, Charles K. 'Managing management' *Special Libraries* 71, (4) April 1980, p. 216.

17   'Your library's advocates: do you benefit from them?' Berner, Andrew and St. Clair, Guy, eds. *The Best of OPL: Five Years of* The One–Person Library Washington DC, Special Libraries Association, 1990, pp. 48–49.

18   Berner, Andrew 'Thinking about ... surviving the 90s,' *The One–Person Library: A Newsletter for Librarians and Management*, 6, 7, November 1989, p.4.

19   Katayama, Jane H. 'The library committee: how important is it?' *Special Libraries*, 24, (1), 1983 p. 44 .

20   White, Herbert S., *Managing the special library*, Knowledge Industry Publications, White Plains, NY, 1984, p. 104.

21   Sinclair, Dorothy, *The administration of the small public library*, American Library Association, Chicago, Illinois, 1979.

22   Bolef, Doris, 'The special library' In: *The how-to-do-it manual for small libraries*, Bill Katz, ed. Neal–Schuman, New York, 1988.

Chapter Eight

Managing the one-person library: the basics

There are advantages to working in a one–person library. The independence one has as a professional librarian in a one–person environment can be a special inducement to excellence, an incentive many in the workforce do not have. Many organizations, constrained by budgetary restrictions to hiring entry–level personnel for managing the library, capitalize on the appeal of independence to new library–school graduates, which means that many professional librarians now managing one–person operations are in their first professional positions. What should the librarian expect on her first day on the job, or, if in the United Kingdom, the first post after licentiate training has been completed?

The first advice that other one–person librarians would give is that the realities of the situation will have little to do with what she has been taught in graduate school, or if she is not a graduate or chartered librarian, with her prior ideas of what goes on in a library. When one works alone, the entire spectrum of objectives, duties and responsibilities is rearranged – not necessarily a bad thing, of course, but a situation which requires frequent adjustment from the first day of employment onwards. So the first thing for the new employee in a one–person library to remember is simply this: be encouraged. Things are not as overwhelming as they seem, and the theories, goals, ideals and aspirations the new one–person librarian has been nourishing so carefully over the past few years are not to be thrown out. They are simply to be recognized for what they are, and while they are not to be forgotten, one must get on with the business at hand: getting the library up and running for the first day of work.

Once the position has been accepted there is a certain amount of thinking to be done about the job. Obviously some of these considerations will have been made upon applying for the position in the first place, and certainly some of the information will have been brought to the attention of the applicant during the interview process, so that by the first day on the job the librarian will already know something about the objectives of the library, its role within the parent organization, and who uses the library and why.

Determining the specific objectives of the library or information unit, and in the process establishing the role of the librarian, as described in Chapter six, are the first tasks for the new employee in the one–person library. Although this is an ongoing process, particular attention to this matter is imperative at the very beginning of the job, and this exercise is immediately followed by a consideration of the concept of ideal versus non–ideal services in information work. As a graduate or chartered librarian, or as someone with interest in and perhaps previous affiliation with a library, the new staff member has some notions of how a library should be managed and how it should fit into the administrative structure of the parent organization. Usually the new employee does not know exactly how things are, and may well be in a good position to do things differently, with the new enthusiasm and interest that comes with being a new employee. This is not to say that the new librarian will come in and change everything around, for such activity is neither appropriate nor desirable, but this is the time to study the situation, to consider it in connection with previous experience and/or education, and come to some conclusions about how the library should be managed, for very soon after reporting for duty, there is going to be much to assimilate, and it will be some days, perhaps even weeks, before the new one–person library manager can get back to thinking about the ideal goals and directions he is interested in bringing to the library.

Ideal vs. non–ideal services

A word of caution is in order here, simply because the very nature of seeking ideals is risky and can lead to disappointment. In thinking about what the library should be, the new librarian is not necessarily determining to achieve these ideals; we are aware that the very nature of ideals, especially in management, is fraught with danger, simply because we are perhaps setting ourselves up to be disappointed. However, we must recognize these ideals and point our work in that direction because a professional librarian is obliged to do the best he or she can under the circumstances. In this context, a consideration of the ideal in library planning is an important part of Dorothy Sinclair's exposition of the planning process. Sinclair is advising the administrator of a small public library, but the concepts are appropriate for any one–person library:

> The librarian must plan at several levels. At the top, not forgotten though temporarily shelved, is the vision of the ideal service for the community. It is wise to start here, before returning to solid realities, for several reasons. The first is that the librarian should never lose his or her vision or high standards, never be content with compromises. Economy may be a necessity, but complacency is the enemy of all progress.
>
> A second reason for considering the ideal before grappling with the feasible is that the ideal may not be as unattainable as it at first appears. Perhaps there is a way to reach the quality of service the community should have. Unless this possibility is considered and all avenues explored, how can the librarian be sure? Even if the service contemplat-

ed in the vision is far off, it is closer than if no vision existed.

In the third place, an ideal pattern is important for present planning. Without long–range goals, current decisions may be shortsighted. Definite, attainable stages in the progress toward long–range goals can be set, and pride can be taken in the realization of these intermediate objectives. The trustees, staff and community share in the excitement of such accomplishments without the danger of settling back into complacency and self–satisfaction after partial success.[1]

The librarian going into a one–person library for the first time, especially if he or she has never worked in a one–person library before, will find a few interesting features which are not often found elsewhere. For example, if the incumbent librarian is to be on duty for a few final days to give the new librarian guidance and direction, not only is the new person going to be caught up in the unusual working conditions of an employee's leaving, but she will be left alone for some of the time because the other librarian simply does not have the time to stop and actually work with the new person. On the other hand, if the incumbent librarian has left the position and the new librarian comes into an empty office, again she will have some time to become oriented to the new situation. It is in the learning time that the new librarian must look around, take stock of the situation and proceed to learn what she can about the library and the work that is to be done there. Quite frankly, no new job ever appears as good as it seemed in the interviews. There are always little surprises, some of them rather nasty, and the new librarian in the one–person library needs to be prepared for them and not be discouraged.

When the surprises come, the first thing to do is to consider what the job will be like after some time has passed, in terms of improvements in service, a different atmosphere in the library, perhaps a new or different attitude toward users, and the like. The new librarian, taking this approach, will be able to see the job as one of challenge and opportunity rather than one of drudgery. It will be necessary to set a few basic rules (a task to be done as pleasantly as possible), as some of the users and other staff in the parent organization will try to test the new employee. One of the oldest gambits, for example, is to ask the new librarian to do a typing job or other task which is not only not in the purview of the librarian but which would not be an appropriate request in any case. Such a request, even from management, will be accompanied by an insinuation that the previous librarian did this work, or that any reasonable person could not possibly object. A firm but pleasant refusal is called for; at the very least, the new librarian will simply reply that, as a new staff member with so many duties not even yet defined, it would be impossible to take on an outside task at this time. This must be established early on, or the librarian will end up doing work she was not hired for and the work of the library will be hindered.

First considerations

There are three areas of interest which the new librarian needs to consider in the early days, and it is important that they be not forgotten in the myriad other concerns being addressed at the same time. In any new library position, but perhaps more so in the one–person library, the daily duties for the first few weeks seem to be staggering in number and complexity, and it is easy for the new librarian to forget that there are broader areas which must be given some thought. The three immediate things to keep in mind are:

- what has gone before
- the library's immediate needs
- planning for the future

In this context, the new librarian in the one–person library should think of himself or herself as an in–house consultant hired to study the library and determine what can be done to make its work more efficient and productive, and at the same time learn how to carry out the regular duties of managing the regular and routine work. As a consultant, the librarian will, in a very short time, have a solid grasp of the work of the library and be in a position to guide its future development.

To determine what has gone before will be the easiest of these three broad tasks, for the librarian's predecessors will have left clues for the new person to follow. In addition, users will be quick to help the one–person librarian learn some of the procedures. Also, of course, one's supervisor and the library committee and board (if there is one), will all be helpful in describing what the library was like prior to the arrival of the new manager. A considerable amount of tact and discretion is required here, for despite possibly obvious inefficiencies, the previous librarian might have been a favourite employee or special friend of some of the users. Equally, the predecessor may have been an excellent librarian about whom no-one had any complaints, but who had a different style from the new librarian. In any case, what we are talking about here is simple courtesy on the job, and while it will probably be necessary to make some decisions to do things differently, one must move slowly and with a certain amount of consideration for those who had become accustomed to the library and the way it was managed before the new person arrived.

Having spent some time analysing previous procedures, the new one–person librarian is in a unique position to study what needs to be done, both in the short– and long–term future. Immediate needs will become apparent almost from the first day, when the copying machine, for example, is found to be located on another floor, despite the fact that the regular copying of journal articles is a standard service offered by the library, and the amount of time and energy consumed in going back and forth to do the copying is a large drain on efficiency. The former librarian may have had no choice in this matter (he or she may have been running the library when there was *no* copying machine) and if the amount of time spent in this way had become onerous by the time that person had decided to leave, it was an appropriate problem to leave for the new librarian. Many such situations will come up in the daily routine, some of which can be corrected immediately and some of which will need to be discussed with management and/or the library committee or board. The first few weeks in the job are not the best time to make drastic recommendations or changes, even if only perceived as such, unless the issues have been carefully discussed prior to employment and the new librarian has a clear mandate to proceed, as well as an assurance of support for any changes that have been agreed upon. Otherwise, it is better to go slowly, to observe carefully and to correct what can be corrected without causing too much disruption, and to save the big battles for later, after the new librarian has built up a reputation for cooperation, efficiency and a pleasant attitude. By setting the stage carefully, the new one–person librarian will find management and the library committee or board receptive to change when the time comes to seek it.

Planning

There is one area where management and the library committee can be approached, after a short period of study and adjustment, and that is the area of planning. Before the new one–person librarian can provide that excellence of service she has agreed to provide, thought must be given to planning. This is very important when working alone, but, sadly, it is the one activity which is most neglected, to the eventual detriment of the quality of service.

The value of the planning process was best set out by G. Edward Evans. We plan because:

1. Planning conserves time, a critical factor in any organization. Developing workable plans requires a great deal of time and effort. Carrying out activities also requires a great deal of time. Employees at all levels are confronted with a dilemma – how to find time to carry out the duties required and still have time to plan. Something always seems to be shortchanged in the pressure to do everything. Sometimes there are too many things to do and too few people. More often, however, it comes back to a problem of poor planning. If intelligent plans are drawn up at the outset, taking into account the resources available, there will be time to plan. Time for planning will have been included in the original plan because it is so critical for continued success.

2. Planning is the only way to combat uncertainty and accommodate environmental changes. Some managers, and many librarians, are willing to sit back and wait for lightning to strike before they make any move ... When supervisors do not examine their operations, and do not plan for some of the more obvious adverse situations that could develop, they

will spend too much time dealing with little problems. Work flow may be efficient at the time procedures are set up, but as time goes on the efficiency may fall off because of changing needs.

3.   Planning focuses attention on organizational objectives. Even when planning is poorly done, it cannot be carried out without some consideration of basic objectives ... In many organizations the real objectives of the organization are lost in the haste to 'do the real work', the day–to–day procedures that are easily understood and rather easily performed. Staff members may begin to resist the need to go back to and examine objectives, because they feel this interferes with the real purposes and function that they perform.

4.   Planning is a critical element in gaining an economical, efficient operation. Planning as a procedure–formulation activity requires consideration of the efficiency and consistency with which work is being performed. It directs the efforts of the organization to achieve a coordinated work flow, and it helps to reduce the number of snap judgements that are made.

5.   Planning is a major factor in the control of the organization. Plans provide the standards by which to measure performance, to ensure that the organization is going in the direction that it is supposed to be going.

Whether the one–person librarian is accustomed to it or not, he must set aside a certain amount of time each week to plan ahead. This can only be time well spent, and it will result in increased productivity and efficiency, thus increasing motivation and job satisfaction. One complaint among one–person librarians is that there is never time to draw breath, much less plan for future activities. Indeed, some one–person librarians complain regularly that there is no time to think about purposes and goals. This attitude in itself is self–defeating, for the librarian who does not engage in some forward planning is doomed to provide a service that is inefficient and counter–productive. The service will not be cost–effective and will not change with the needs of the organization, and the library itself will be top–heavy with out–of–date material which has not been discarded or even organized in the first place. The administration of any small library, and most especially a one–person library, requires that time be available not only for the required day–to–day professional effort but for planning as well.

During the first few months of the job, the new librarian managing a one–person operation will soon begin to discern what the real goals are (as opposed to the stated or perceived goals, which might be different) for the users, the management, and the committee or board if there is one. It is possible that these goals might vary considerably, and the new librarian will find herself, as in-house consultant, preparing a strategic plan for the library, to describe what the library might be doing for its users and the organization it supports. Such plans are not uncommon, and generally look at information services in terms of five, ten or even fifteen years. Such a plan will require time for interviews with users, perhaps some special meetings with management and committee personnel, and certainly some quiet time for thinking about the ideal library situation and the situation as it is at present. Thought must be given to such areas as sympathetic management, resources for the anticipated programmes, and financial support for providing at least minimal services (including proper equipment, lighting, space, furniture, etc.). The librarian working alone will be forced to spend a certain amount of his personal time thinking about these subjects, and after they have been studied and discussed with all appropriate parties, a document will be drawn up and presented to both management and the committee. Such a document, the library's strategic plan, will not only give the one-person librarian direction for his efforts over the next few years but will enhance the reputation and value of the librarian with users, management, committee and board members, and others in the organization.

Limitations

Nevertheless, without undermining the importance of planning, it is appropriate to return to Dorothy Sinclair, for in addition to providing guidance in the planning process, Sinclair offers another principle which can be appropriated for the one-person library, regardless of type: 'Perhaps the most important matter for the consideration of the board and administrator of the small library is this matter of limitations. What shall this particular library try to do and be?'[1]

Limitations are something none of us is particularly interested in addressing, primarily because, as practitioners in a service profession which many enter in order to help people, to guide users to the information they need, and even, when called upon, to help them interpret the material, we do not like to think of ourselves as denying any request. However, no library can be all things to all people, and none tries. Equality of service to all users is an important aspect of providing a service in most libraries. However, in the single staff library (where the librarian is short of time and resources) this is not always possible to achieve. The librarian, instead, must prioritize her work in order to meet the information needs of the company or institution. For example, if the Financial Director of the company requires a set of economic statistics for an important Board meeting, this request must be dealt with as a matter of urgency by the librarian. But if another member of staff wants to know why her favourite houseplant looks unwell, then the librarian should suggest politely that she head to her nearest public library. In this way, the resources of the library are being directed towards the needs of the Company and the Directors. A librarian who is politically aware will ensure that this service is first class as the Director ultimately decides on the allocation of finance to the Library. Even the New York Public Library, the British Library, the Library of Congress, and other major research institutions have subject areas in which they do not collect. While limitations are not such a serious problem in the business or corporate library (probably because they were created and designed for specific purposes), in the library of a museum or historical society or other cultural institution, it is not uncommon for the library to attempt to provide broad coverage of many subject areas which are not unique to their collecting interests. The limitations of a library, especially one small enough to be managed by one person, are not cause for apology. Indeed, by limiting what they do, one–person libraries are often able to do things better than some of the larger institutions which try to do too much.

The service principle

The one–person librarian is employed to provide information services. Within the financial constraints established by the supporting organization, her role is to determine the best methods of providing the highest standards of excellent service.

On the other hand, the one–person librarian is not employed primarily to do the many things that she must do simply to keep the library going. The administrative functions can (and will) be turned over to someone else when they interfere with service. In the one–person library, service is noticeably personal and special. It is not servile, and should not be provided from a subservient point of view: it is a service provided by a professional library manager who has the skills and abilities that make her an asset to the parent organization; so much so that without that personalized and special service, the work of the parent organization could not be done. The responsibilities of the one–person librarian are indeed built around her organization of the collection, but that organization is complemented and enhanced by her special skill in providing personalized service.

For the one–person librarian, one of the major appeals of the work is the diversity of duties. One never hears such an employee complaining of being bored with his job, simply because the demands on time and energy are so many and so varied that there is no opportunity to be bored. The duties of the one–person librarian can be categorized in a number of ways, but the method most often chosen is to describe those tasks which are user services and those connected with support services. While the time devoted to the latter is often considerably out of proportion to that spent on the former, it is the user services which define the one–person librarian's job.

User services in the one–person library can be: circulation (the lending of books, periodicals and other library materials), request services, scanning and routing periodicals, and SDI (selective dissemination of information, in which the librarian reviews the literature, filters from it items of significance and sends these directly to various individuals according to their stated interests), photocopying, interlibrary loan activity, abstracting, indexing, performing electronic or manual searches, information and reference work, and project work and report writing. All of these are services offered for users and must be provided efficiently, accurately and quickly. Support services are those library activities which the one–person librarian must perform when he or she is not working with a user, and these are the ones that provide the organization and efficiency required for successful library management. They include book ordering and the necessary research involved classifying and cataloguing the collection, internal accounting procedures, administrative tasks due to the library's affiliation with the supporting organization (as well as administrative tasks involved in working with the committee or board), and, of course, keeping loan records, reservation requests, shelving, labelling, filing and the many other 'little' tasks which, when left undone, can seriously hamper the efficient operation of the library.

These support services are not the only ones, but in the one–person library there are other duties which, if possible, should always be contracted out. They include journal subscription order and fulfilment, book and journal binding, conservation and restoration work, secretarial tasks (typing, correspondence etc.) when there is a secretary in another department whose services can be used by the library, and any printing which has to be done for the library (accession lists, guides, annual reports etc.).

Professional and clerical tasks

It can be seen that the traditional concept of the librarian solely as a custodian of books is no longer applicable, for today's librarian is a master of many tasks. A librarian/information specialist in a one–person library must be a generalist. When we look at the tasks listed for user and support services it is not difficult to see that the librarian in the one–person library must be able to do a little of everything. This librarian may have to abstract, index, catalogue and classify books and journals, perform literature searches manually, online or by teletext, scan and route literature, compile bibliographies and reading lists, write reports and assess information found in the searches performed. In addition to these tasks, usually called 'professional' because they require special education and skills, the librarian in a one–person library must handle the myriad clerical tasks that keep the library running smoothly. Reference queries (another professional task for which special education is required) also must be answered, and the modern qualified librarian may regard the library much more as an information centre, containing as much non–book material as actual shelved books.

In the world of libraries and librarianship there is much discussion about the distinctions between clerical and professional work. It is commonly agreed that professional work requires special education, skills and abilities, and the library employee who has attained the status of graduate librarian (in the United States) or chartered librarian (in the United Kingdom) is generally accorded the distinction of being a 'professional.' His or her duties in the one–person library are going to be the user services and management which require the special ability achieved with graduate study. On the other hand, many of the tasks described above certainly do not require special education and ability. The skills for completing these tasks are generally called 'clerical.' The question thus arises: should a professional librarian be doing clerical work? Conversely, should a clerical employee be doing professional work? Or should a professional librarian refuse a position in a one–person library, on the grounds that he or she does not perform clerical work?

The answer cannot be a simple yes or no, for the decision is not the librarian's to make. The distinction between professional and clerical tasks is one made within the library and information services profession. While it certainly affords all of us, pragmatists and theoreticians alike, the opportunity to express our opinion that the ideal library will have a minimum staff of two employees – a professional librarian and a support person – the realities of the workplace are such that one–person libraries not only currently exist but will continue to exist. Despite the strenuous efforts of many in the library and information services profession, business managers and human resources personnel are not always concerned with *our* distinctions between clerical and professional tasks. This attitude, of course, often leads to the conclusion that a single employee will be sufficient for the job. No matter how much the practitioners might want to separate 'professional' from 'clerical' tasks, and to have each performed by appropriate personnel, management makes the final decisions based on its own perceptions.

Finally, however, the question is moot, for in the one–person library there is no choice. When there is only one person to do the work the distinction between clerical and professional is really no longer relevant. We admit that non–professional tasks consume a great deal of time for professional, chartered librarians – time which could otherwise be used in performing, at a higher level, many of the professional tasks that are not done as well as the librarian would like. At the same time, we are obliged to recognize that many employees who manage one–person libraries are not graduate or chartered librarians, for the economies of many of the organizations which often most need the services of a staff member do not permit hiring a trained professional. Thus we have to conclude that the major difference between professional work and clerical tasks in a one–person library is determined by one's attitude. How the librarian feels about the work he or she is doing becomes much more important than whether this task is clerical or that one professional. In the one–person library the employee is required to provide his or her own professional affirmation. Thus, the one–person librarian must think of himself or herself as a professional sometimes doing clerical work, not as a clerk working in a library. The standard of service in the library requires it, and the librarian, as an employee making a contribution to the parent organization and its goals, must accept nothing less.

Paraprofessional and non-professional support

For some, lack of time to get everything done is thought to be the biggest problem for the one–person librarian. While a case can be made that a properly structured library can be operated by one person (depending, of course, on such factors as size of collection, requests for services, level of reference or research services etc.), there are a number of situations in which the librarian cannot in fact get all the work done and will require some form of additional support. Such tasks as an annual inventory, the disposal of non–current, unretained periodicals, preparations for the occasional book sale or other special event in the library, or the shifting of a sizeable collection all require more manpower than one person can supply.

Temporary staff

If the parent organization is large enough that there is a personnel 'pool' upon which various departments can draw for special projects and assignments, this is the obvious source of temporary help. If such employees are not available, the one–person librarian must approach management for funding for some kind of temporary employee, obtained through the librarian's own contacts or through a company or institutional personnel department. In either case, it is the one–person librarian who must determine when additional support staff is required and then make a case for hiring the employee. The request itself is made in terms of the requirements for continued library service, and not as a special favour. The need for staff must be explained clearly, demonstrating precisely that the work to be done will result in better service.

Student assistants

The classic approach to obtaining inexpensive help in the library has been the use of student assistants. Long accepted in secondary–school libraries and in college and university libraries, student assistants have been utilized in almost every non–professional capacity. Even small departmental libraries in universities have no compunction about hiring student help, and the trend has now become so popular that we see student assistants (often referred to as 'general assistants') being utilized in small corporate, museum, church and synagogue, healthcare agency and law libraries. The reason is obvious: student help is cheap. Beatrice Sichel considered student employees, and while she lists several advantages for having students on the library staff, the primary one is financial. The substantial differential in the compensation offered a permanent staff member and a temporary student worker 'can be a serious budgetary consideration, particularly since fringe benefits, including paid holidays, vacation time, sick leave, contributions to insurance and retirement plans, and longevity bonuses increase the compensation costs for permanent employees 22.6%. When this is contrasted with the costs for student assistants, who generally find the minimum hourly wage acceptable, the advantages of student help are obvious.'[3]

There are other advantages to having a student on the staff, one being, as Sichel points out, that student staff are useful in keeping the library open for more hours than would be possible with only one person on the staff – a benefit that many libraries in small hospitals utilize. For the one–person librarian, however, the primary advantage of having a student on the staff, even if only for 5 or 10 hours a week, is having someone to help with the routine tasks. A good student assistant can be taught to shelve materials, sort reports and pamphlets, file, and generally assist in the myriad duties which accumulate, and even paraprofessional tasks such as shelf reading and inventory checking can be given over to a well-trained and conscientious student assistant. The very fact that there are duties, even occasional ones, which the librarian does not have to perform and can give to someone else do, can be a tremendous morale boost for the librarian in charge of a one–person library.

Prepractitioners
In the United Kingdom, any candidate wishing to enter the list of Licentiates of the Library Association must fulfil certain conditions, one of which is to have undergone a period of supervised post examination training under a chartered librarian who is on the Register of the Library Association. This training programme lasts for one year and enables the trainee to gain practical experience in professional work. In the United States, the procedures are less formal, but it is common practice for students in graduate schools of library and information science to participate in supervised work-study programmes (the difference being that in the United States these are undertaken while the student is enrolled in graduate school, not after the studies are completed).

There is a variety of objectives to this arrangement, and they seem equally beneficial regardless of where they are practised:

- To introduce the person to the professional working environment

- To enable the person to gain experience in professional practice in order to complement the theory studied in graduate school

- To give the person an opportunity to gain knowledge of the wide range of work available within the profession

- To enable the person to gain new skills and knowledge

- To provide the person with opportunities for professional and personal development

- To develop in the person attitudes to professional work which reflect high professional standards

Such programmes can be a source of additional support for one–person libraries, as long as the librarian agrees that the student is there to learn to become a professional practitioner. The one–person librarian who decides to use such staff must be willing to make a commitment to train and supervise the employee, but in this case the librarian has the advantage of knowing that the student is interested in the job and already has a level of professional expertise not always found in other temporary employees.

Volunteers

In the not–for–profit sector, volunteers are often looked to as an additional source of staff, but in most communities labour laws (or unwritten rules, in some cases) require that those who volunteer their services cannot be asked to perform tasks for which the library should be hiring paid employees. Such tasks as inventory, shifting books etc. are not appropriate for people who are giving their time and energies, because these tasks are part of the business of running a library. The library and its parent organization must be prepared to pay a fair wage to have these tasks performed. On the other hand, tasks (usually those which might not be considered absolutely essential by management or supervisory personnel but which would enable the library to provide better service) can be assigned to volunteers, who when properly trained and supervised, can make a significant contribution to the library's work. Such tasks as sorting and arranging archival materials, preparing simple descriptive bibliographies for certain collections, sitting at reception desks, answering the telephone etc., can be handled by trained volunteers. Guidelines for using volunteers are available from the American Library Association[5] and Harold Jenkins has written a useful article which spells out many of the advantages and disadvantages of using volunteers.[6] The best guide, however, came out in 1983 in the form of a special report on volunteers. Prepared by Alice Sizer Warner, *Volunteers in Libraries II* is a basic text which dispels many of our preconceived ideas about volunteers and their use, simply because Warner's guidance is based on information she received from some 700 respondents to questionnaires mailed to libraries of all types and sizes. She sees the growth of volunteerism as a natural phenomenon of the 1980s, which she describes as a decade that brought with it '...a political atmosphere where macroeconomics is having visible and often drastic effects on mini (and not so mini) libraries. "Volunteerism" is now not only the wonderful pioneer pitch–in spirit, it is the unwritten law of the land.'[7]

Warner asserts that there is agreement today that 'the single most important reason for a volunteer programme is public relations', and people come to the library to work as volunteers for a variety of reasons: civic responsibility, need for structure in their schedules, the desire to meet new people, to obtain hands–on job experience, especially to have references they can use when looking for jobs, to get out of the house and, frankly, because they are bored, to fill time in their lives, to do something active in retirement.[7]

Can a volunteer programme be of use to the one–person librarian? No single answer can work for all one–person libraries, but before plunging into such a programme to obtain people to help with some of the jobs that just do not seem to get done, there are a few basic guidelines which Warner offers:

> The first step, for any library bent on careful exploration of whether and how to use volunteers, is carefully to define and review the goals of the library. Is the library accomplishing what it has set out to do? If not, what are alternative, feasible ways of reaching goals? Might a volunteer labor force be a workable solution?

> It is a good idea to gather as much information as possible about how other libraries, particularly libraries either nearby or approximately the same size, are using volunteers. Also, in early planning stages, a look should be taken to see if there already exists a community organization devoted to helping with volunteers and to finding and prescreening volunteers.[7]

The one–person librarian should also ask himself if there is enough work, and whether the volunteers would help or hinder the efficient operation of the library. Will the public relations gains be worth the effort that goes into working with volunteers? If the answers are negative, the librarian will do better to look elsewhere for extra help.

References

1 Sinclair, Dorothy, *The Administration of the Small Public Library*, American Library Association, Chicago, 1979, p. 9.

2 Evans, G. Edward, *Management Techniques for Librarians*, Academic Press, New York,1976.

3 Sichel, Beatrice, 'Utilizing student assistants in small libraries,' *Journal of Library Administration*, 3, (1),1982, p. 36.

4 Manpower Services Commission, *The Youth Training Scheme* (Details from the Manpower Services Commission, Moorfoot, Sheffield, UK).

5 American Library Association, Library Administration Division, 'Guidelines for using volunteers in libraries,' *American Libraries*, 2, April, 1971, pp. 407-408.

6 Jenkins, Harold. 'The library volunteer: volunteers in the future of libraries,' *Library Journal*, 97, 15 April, 1972, pp. 1399-1403.

7 Warner, Alice Sizer, *Volunteers in Libraries II*, Library Journal Special Report #24, Bowker, New York, 1983, p.4.

Chapter Nine

Self-management and time management in the one-person library

The list of duties in a one-person library is enormous. Not only is the librarian responsible for the full range of professional duties, such as readers' advisory, answering reference questions, selecting and ordering material, cataloguing and classification, collection review and similar tasks, but he or she must also fit clerical duties into the schedule, including typing, filing, circulation counts, shelving etc. Even occasional custodial duties such as cleaning shelves or shifting books are often done by the librarian, who quickly learns that the fastest way to get something done is to do it herself. To do *all* these jobs and do them well requires a level of self–management that none of us is taught in graduate school, and few of us learn even later. It is easy to say we can manage our time, especially if we are part of a staff and duties are defined; but it is difficult when everything must be done by one person. There are no rules imposed by management, there are no time-sheets, there are no supervisors looking over one's shoulder.

The key to self-management is to establish priorities. There are certain jobs in every library which must be dutifully performed, otherwise a backlog accumulates and what has been a daily routine can quickly become a monumental project. So the first rule of self-management in a one-person library is obvious: get the housekeeping done first, do it early each day and get it out of the way. The librarian who skips the circulation count on Monday will find herself with twice as much to count on Tuesday, and Monday's efficiency will be reduced by worrying about not having done it.

A second rule continues the establishment of priorities: concentrate the effort on those activities which call for immediate action. Of course, the choice is obvious if one is deciding between answering a reference enquiry or working on the index to the organization's archives. The librarian must answer the enquiry first. However, he will be aware that producing the index is a valid and professional activity, and the conscientious one-person librarian will try to find some time each day for precisely this type of work. This choice is easy. It is more difficult when the librarian must choose between two equally essential tasks. This is where one's professionalism is called upon. The librarian's experience and background will enable him to establish proper professional priorities.

In all libraries, there are professional duties which call for an immediate response, such a readers' advisory and reference. However, many tasks in a library are not so pressing, but upon completion they will enable the librarian to respond to requests for immediate information more successfully. These are valid professional activities and the librarian should be aware of them, of their demands on his time and their eventual contribution to the library operation. He does not need to apologize for such activities, and even if they are so esoteric that only the librarian will know about them and use them, they are nevertheless part of the job and he should feel a responsibility to plan time for such activities; the service to the users will be better for it.

Once determined, specific work in every library must be considered in such a way as to be performed effectively and efficiently. Unfortunately, many people often approach their tasks entirely wrongly, with the common approach being to achieve, complete and remove the task, whereas the first thing should be to plan the task and think about how it should be completed. While planning in its broadest sense was discussed earlier, it is suggested here as one of several approaches to self-management and time management. Probably the best way to do this is by using the systems approach, particularly suitable for a small library because the librarian is often entrusted with two jobs – the collection and storage of materials and the exploitation of those materials on behalf of the library users.

To begin with, there are two questions to ask when setting up or running a small library. First, what are the basic informational requirements of the organization? Second, how can these requirements best be satisfied with the existing resources? It is a commonly accepted notion in the profession that many library systems came about because a member of management 'thought it was a good idea at the time'. It cannot be stressed enough how wrong this thinking is, because an arbitrarily chosen system can have more influence on the library operation than the real requirements. Thus systems planning requires that you discover the real needs of the organization before you set up or reorganize the library. Often, because of lack to time to think through the potential need and uses for a library service, the service provided is unrelated to the users' actual requirements. For instance, management might have an uninformed understanding – or misunderstanding – of the services a library can provide, perhaps perceiving a library simply as a book-ordering service, and not being aware that the requirements of the organization could be better served by the use of online databases combined with the use of document delivery services to supply the materials themselves. Management might never have thought of an SDI service, or considered how it could benefit the staff. In short, you must put a great deal of thought into the planning of a small library service, and you must be able to convince management that traditional systems are not necessarily the best as far as cost-effectiveness and time saving are concerned. It is thinking and planning for these eventualities which makes them happen, and while the one-person librarian is carrying out her daily tasks it is also imperative that she be engaged in a continuous thinking and planning process.

Self-management, then, begins with the establishment of priorities. It also requires a high level of self-motivation. For the librarian in a one-person library, there is no choice but to be highly motivated, because he or she has no one else to turn to (or blame, when things go wrong). Every decision must be made in terms of 'How can *I* accomplish this task' or 'How does this fit into *my* schedule of activities?' There may be several choices of how to perform a particular task, but the one-person librarian limits the choices to those which get the job done most quickly and most efficiently.

It is this self-motivation which leads to the unconventional entrepreneurial spirit so typical in small organizations. The one-person librarian has to know just who to turn to when his own resources are not sufficient for the task in hand, and he needs to know (and to justify) managerial support for outside expenditures, for new technology, for labour-saving devices, for the exploitation of external resources. Often, in fact, the librarian has to know how and when to seek support elsewhere, and when to go around management and find another way to get what is needed. Obviously the use of networks and connections is a primary example of this kind of thinking, for one-person librarians must be expert at knowing who has the information (or a lead to the information) his or her user might be seeking. This is the kind of thing the one-person librarian must be constantly thinking about – how to manage successfully with whatever resources are available, and the stimulus for finding and using these resources must come from the librarian herself. The one-person librarian, more than any other library administrator, must be an entrepreneur.

Time management

The basic concepts of time management have been identified by a number of experts. In 1966, in the now classic (and still eminently valuable) *The Effective Executive*, Peter Drucker identified the keys to effective time management: effective executives do not start with their tasks:

> They start with time.... They start by finding out where their time actually goes. Then they attempt to manage their time and to cut back unproductive demands on their time. Finally they consolidate their 'discretionary' time into the largest possible continuing units. This three-step process:
>
> * recording time
>
> * managing time
>
> * consolidating time
>
> is the foundation of executive effectiveness.[1]

The first step, then, for the one-person librarian who is attempting to manage her time is to look at how time is used. Time logs, recording such things as goals, activities during the day, the amount of time each activity required to complete, and similar data, can be an especially useful management tool for the one-person librarian. A time log is nothing more than a record of how the librarian uses her time, and while opinion varies about the value of an ongoing daily time log, there is no question that an occasional recording of one's activities – usually of three days' duration – can be beneficial. By keeping a time log several times a year, in order to take advantage of seasonal variations, the one-person librarian puts herself in the position of *knowing* where the time is going. And since most people are not aware of the strong disparity between how they *think* they use their time and how they actually use it, the one-person librarian is usually surprised at the amount of time devoted to non-essential or marginal activities.

In addition to knowing how one uses one's time, it is also necessary for the one-person librarian to know how to manage time, and it is here that we come to the sticky question of individual values. For one librarian, a quick-answer telephone reference query might be a time-wasting interruption, while for another, it is the reason he is there. On the other hand, if the parameters of the library's services have been clearly established, the librarian early on learns which demands on his time are valid and which are inappropriate. The task then becomes one of determining how best to meet the legitimate demands on one's time while at the same time – despite risking misunderstandings on the part of others in the community or organization – eliminating or minimizing the inappropriate activities. When we add to this the fact that in one-person libraries, librarians must, as Andrew Berner so succinctly put it, 'be prepared to undertake a large amount of 'office work' in addition to their higher mission of providing information for users',[2] the value of a time-management programme for a one-person library is established.

Goal setting

For popular management consultant Michael LeBoeuf, effectiveness begins with goal setting[3] For the one-person librarian, LeBoeuf's guidelines for setting goals can be a useful time-management tool, and his first rule – that goals must be challenging but attainable – is basic in the management of a one-person library. The person who is in charge of providing library services without assistance will find herself stretching to make the service better, to accommodate as many users as possible, and at the same time, to accomplish her goals within the parameters that she and management together have set for the service. For example, it might seem to be a reasonable goal for the one-person library in a small museum to acquire a rare collection of early 20th-century French art periodicals, and the librarian, who happens to be interested in the subject, might positively dream about the idea. But the practicalities of such a purchase, even if a set should come on the market at a price the museum could pay, would seriously hamper the operations of the library, because of acquisitions procedures and security considerations, to say nothing of the additional demands on the librarian's time while he organized and catalogued the collection. The goal of becoming a major resource centre for the subject might well be a challenging one, but in real terms it is not attainable as long as the parameters of service in the library are limited to those which can be provided by one professional employee.

Another of LeBoeuf's guidelines requires that the librarian's goals be as specific and measurable as possible. It is easy for a one-person library manager to say that she is going to become a better librarian: an admirable goal indeed, and one with which few would argue. But can it be done? Not until she has determined measurable criteria for being a 'better' librarian ('I will take a course in time management', say, or 'I will eliminate the unprocessed reports backlog.') can she approach her original goal. In doing so, the criteria themselves become the goals, with the resulting effect that she has, through accomplishing those measurable activities, become what she set out to be, 'a better librarian.'

In choosing goals for the effective management of the one-person library, compatibility of goals is a requirement. It is not difficult to set two goals which in the planning stages seem perfectly sensible but which in practice cancel each other out and cause considerable stress and confusion. This situation often occurs in the corporate setting, where there is an organizational policy that materials will be available in the information centre for research. The librarian, in an attempt to offer the most complete library service possible, encourages various staff members to sign up for a journal-routing system on the assumption that the journals will be quickly scanned and then routed to the next person on the list, ending up back in the library in a very short time. Of course this is not the way things happen, and the librarian, in his desire to establish a visible and useful service, forgets about the human element, the fact that people will be away from their desks, or that they will keep the journal until they have read a long article in it, and so forth. Both goals, the desire to have a journal-routing service and the policy to have journals in the library for research, are admirable, but they cancel each other out. They are not compatible.

Finally, goals must be flexible or, in LeBoeuf's terms, 'forever evolving'. Consequently they must be reevaluated, modified, sometimes discarded and sometimes replaced. For the hospital librarian whose goal of quality service has been to provide hard copy of all periodicals requested more frequently than some standard number of times a year, the rising costs of scientific periodicals and the proximity of libraries with collections available to information brokers and document-delivery services has required her to change her thinking. While it might be less cumbersome to have a particular periodical title on site, this one-person library is not a major research library and the administrative requirements of ordering, acquiring, processing, binding and shelving the journals are no longer appropriate in this setting. Times have changed, and now the costs of using an information broker and a document-delivery service are far less than the costs of acquiring the titles, so she just doesn't do it. Her institution cannot afford the money and she cannot afford the time, so her goals for quality service have changed. Cost has replaced convenience as her primary criterion for setting this particular goal.

Attitude

Time management, as it relates to one-person librarianship, essentially involves a consideration of one or more steps toward self-improvement, which in itself requires more than just a recognition of the need and a willingness to apply oneself to the task. It also requires an ordered system within which the most important aspects of work can be incorporated and actions taken. When reduced to its most basic level, effective time management includes three fundamental factors:

- Recognition of the need
- Desire to do something about the need
- Well-managed time to allow action to occur

Essentially good time management means reorganizing your approach to your work. We have already stressed the importance of planning and thinking, which must be included in one's daily activities. You do not have to look busy all the time. Take time to stop and think about what you are doing or what needs to be done. This alone will reap dividends.

Ian Barclay, lecturer in the Department of Industrial Studies at Liverpool University, suggests one approach to time management:

- Attitude to your job tasks
- Approach to your job tasks
- Analysis of your activities
- Application of techniques
- Appraisal of effect
- Enjoyment of achieving the goal[4]

In discussing attitude we should keep in mind that personal characteristics have much to do with time management. By understanding your personality and how it influences how you use your time you can take steps to maximize the beneficial aspects and minimize the detrimental ones. Examples include your self-image, your ability to build on your strengths (and minimize your weaknesses), your approach to your work, whether you are an introvert or an extrovert, whether your are a morning person or a night owl, and similar characteristics in your personality that affect your performance and your productivity. If you are aware of these characteristics, you can make them work for you.

Task components also influence your use of time. You might be spending a disproportionate amount of time on tasks you enjoy, to the detriment of other work. Clearly, the pleasant aspects of the job produce job satisfaction, but you must determine how much time you can justify for doing what you like. One of the basic rules of the workplace is that no job, no matter how perfect it may seem to others, is going to be perfect in practice. There will always be something that is not a favourite thing to do, but which has to be done.

Regardless of how much you like your work, avoid becoming a workaholic. You need your leisure, and you should make sure you get it. You will function better for it, and you will be able to make better decisions if you can clear your mind on a regular basis.

Finally, we recognize that in managing a one-person library, the guidelines for an effective operation are going to be our own. We look everywhere we can for help, and when we come across them, we incorporate them into what we are doing. There is no shortage of self-help rules to get us through the work day alone, but some of the most useful are the following:

- Do not waste time complaining about problems

- Accept your limitations – perfection is not a useful standard in the workplace

- Be friendly to your users

- Keep calm and never panic – no-one can complete a task successfully in a panic situation

- Think about your task more than once if you need to, but only *do* it once

- View problems as opportunities: don't just solve them, exploit them as well

- If you have a problem, do something about it now – don't procrastinate

- Do not pursue lost causes

- Do not make excuses

- Do not say you will try to do something on time – just do it

- Do not look for difficulties – they may never come up

- Start something new each day

- Finish something each day

- Keep outside activities out of work

- Be on time and keep appointments

- Do the hardest jobs first, when your energy is highest

- Use selective delays: stop sometimes and think about the specific job you are doing at the moment

- Use scientific techniques when appropriate

- Do not miss deadlines

- Be honest with yourself and with others – seek help if you do not know how to do something yourself

- Budget well

- Be composed

- Bring any conflict out into the open

- Improve your learning, concentration and reading skills

- Recognize stress and learn how to cope with it

- Avoid substance abuse during the work day

- Stay fit

- Develop a confidant or mentor – you need someone to talk to

- Don't be lazy

- Avoid negative or destructive thinking

- Recognize that you can do more than one thing at a time

- Ask others how they manage time

Interruptions vs. service

Management procedures and productivity are considerably compromised in the one-person library. If Drucker's third key to management success is the consolidation of time, how on earth, one might ask, is the one-person librarian expected to work in larger blocks of time, when most of his or her work comes in bits and pieces as users bring themselves to the library or call it for information? While the common goal in the library and information services profession is to provide information to specified user group, in fact the one-person library manager, attempting to provide those services at the same time as managing a businesslike and efficient office, is often put in the awkward position of deciding what she is: is she an information provider, always on call, or is she an office manager, implementing policies and procedures which themselves lead to the successful achievement of the library's mission?

For the committed and conscientious one-person librarian, of course, there is no choice. He is there to serve his users, and he must be prepared to interrupt any task in order to respond to a query. Having said that, however, there are techniques and approaches that can be suggested for alleviating some of the stress that interruptions bring.

The first thing is to learn to distinguish between what we call 'legitimate' interruptions and 'illegitimate' ones. In calling ourselves 'library and information services professionals', the key word is 'services'. Librarianship is a service profession, and our very reason for being is to serve our users, to meet their information needs so that they can do what they need to do with that information. Therefore, any 'interruption' which comes about as a result of a user seeking information from the librarian is not an interruption at all, or, if we choose to be strict about it, it is a 'legitimate' interruption.

It is the illegitimate interruptions that cause the worst problems, probably because both parties know that such activities are not in the best interests of the work, and from a purely organizational point of view, time spent dealing with such situations is time taken illegitimately from the company or organization. Nevertheless, there are those who do not understand our work and will come to the library to kill time. As library managers, we find ourselves in something of a bind because we want to create an inviting atmosphere in the library, but on the other hand, we have our work to do.

The most appropriate method for dealing with illegitimate requests for our time comes from Jimmy Calano and Jeff Salzman, who are recognized for having created the CareerTracking programmes in America. Their solution?:

> Be ruthless with time wasters... Develop a mind-set that judges every activity in terms of whether it brings you closer, however minutely, to your goals... You'll know when to say no. Even better, other people will tune in to your no-nonsense approach and learn to respect your time as much as you do[5]

There are, of course, time-management considerations even for legitimate interruptions, and such techniques as perfecting one's reference interview skills, keeping the most-used quick-answer reference materials near the telephone, and learning to avoid 'face-saving' responses ('Let me see what I can find' when you know you have nothing on the subject) can be put to good use in the one-person library. Learning to say 'no' is, of course, the hardest thing of all, but there are reasons to avoid wasting time by attempting to respond when you know you cannot provide the correct response. When a user approaches the library with an inappropriate request (seeking business information in a scientific research library, for example, or guidance to take secondhand to a child who is doing a research paper or other school assignment), the tendency for most of us is to make some attempt to help. While this is fine from a societal point of view, it wastes time that should be more appropriately spent on other matters. Therefore, saying 'no' becomes a matter of some importance in the one-person library, and the best guidance for us comes not from the library field but from the time-management literature. Alec Mackenzie and Kay Cronkite Waldo offer four steps for saying 'no' without offending:

- Listen to ensure understanding and convey sympathy: 'I understand your request for research materials on the last battles of the American Civil War'.

- Say no immediately, to eliminate doubt and the guilt which continued discussion engenders: 'No, I can't supply you with any information about that subject'.

- Give reasons so that your refusal can be accepted: 'You may not realize it, but our collection here is limited to information that supports research projects funded within the corporation.'

- Offer alternatives to demonstrate good faith: 'I happen to serve on a committee with the Director of the Historical Society. Let me put you in touch with him.'[6]

One of the most difficult situations for the one-person librarian has to do with finding time to be alone, for it is then that consolidated blocks of time are available. It is frequently necessary to find time for uninterrupted work – time when the librarian will not be required to stop what he or she is doing in order to complete a project or a task. We have to recognize, and train our managers and users to recognize, that there are tasks in the library which must be performed without interruption. While such recognition has some impact on the services we are to provide, in most cases 'always-on-call' library services are not required. Such services have become traditional simply because we as librarians have always seen ourselves as serving as many people as we could within a given time. In fact such service standards are not very practical, for in addition to being unrealistic, they encourage users to develop expectations which cannot reasonably be met.

The first step in dealing with this situation is to determine beforehand which tasks should not be interrupted. If the list is long and the tasks recur regularly, it will be necessary to go to management to establish set hours when the library manager will be on duty to take queries, and times when he will not be available. As the manager of a department in which certain administrative and managerial tasks must be performed, the one-person librarian cannot be expected to provide concentrated labour if it is impossible to concentrate.

Establishing a set time for library services, and a time when library services are not offered, will require a serious and conscientious study of library usage patterns, and it will mean determining which users (if any) might be inconvenienced by a reduction in 'public' or 'open' hours. These hours themselves can be as generous or as limited as necessary, and prior to putting set hours into effect, an information campaign must be carried out to ensure that all users become aware of the library's hours of service. At the same time, if the librarian is going to be on duty during those particular times, he must carefully adhere to that schedule. Otherwise, the scheme will abort and he will be back to being on call at all times.

The next step is to implement some sort of screening mechanism, to ensure that when the librarian is not available, messages can be left for her through a voicemail system, an answering machine, or a receptionist or secretary. Again, the responsibility of the librarian is paramount, for she must be scrupulous about picking up her messages and returning calls on schedule.

There are other techniques for dealing with interruptions and several of these are worth repeating here:

- Set aside a regularly scheduled time for yourself and your work. Accommodate yourself and you'll work better. This can be early in the morning (if you're a morning person), or later at a quiet time during the day, if you can accomplish more then. The important thing is to set aside a quiet time and observe it, as strictly as you would any other appointment on your calendar. It's been suggested that an 'open-door policy' results in one and a half wasted hours each day. Can you afford that?

- Delegate. Yes, even in a one-person library, there might be some things you can ask someone else to do. Is there a typing pool that serves management, but you're typing your own correspondence? Ask if your correspondence can be turned over to that service. What about mail pick-up and delivery, or supplies? Are you going to those work areas while other departments are having their materials picked up and returned by some 'floating' staff? Think about it. There might be some tasks you can delegate (and they are probably activities that interfere with the performance of your professional tasks).

- When you accept a project or a task, finish it. Don't get part-way through and have it hanging over you. Otherwise, you'll find yourself interrupting other work to get this job on its way again.

- Likewise, if it's a document or a piece of paper (or even a reference book), handle it once. Don't pick it up, look at the information you need, put it down, and do something else. Get the information you need, dispose of it, get rid of the document or book, and go on to something else.

- Put things away. Keep one project going on your desk at a time, and, when possible, one book or set of materials off the shelf at one time. Don't pile a lot of stuff around. It doesn't make you look busy—it makes you look disorganized, and it creates a mess you have to wade through when you want something. And that creates interruptions.

- Don't be too quick to become involved in meetings, socializing and the like. You're not at the office to win any popularity contests, and while we're all social beings and need some time to relax as we go through the day, we have to be on guard constantly to keep the socializing and meetings from becoming too pervasive in our work day.

- Look around the office and see if you are an 'attractive nuisance' to others on the staff who might want to kill a little time with you. Is your desk near a water fountain, restroom, copying machine, or on the way to the staff lounge? Watch that kind of thing, because it's hard to get your work done if everybody passing by has to stop and have a word or two.[7]

Finally, for the one-person library manager there are two more lists of time-management objectives, also from the management field. Drucker's famous 'systematic time management' bears repeating, especially in the light of the work we do in a one-person library:

- Identify and eliminate the things that need not be done at all
- Identify activities which can be done by someone else
- Identify and eliminate activities that waste other people's time[1]

LeBoeuf argues that managers are not only required to have a list of things to do, they must also keep a 'not-to-do-List', activities which must be avoided if the library manager is going to succeed as a time manager:

- All low-priority items – unless the high-priority items have been completed
- Any task whose completion is of little or no consequence. When you have something to do ask yourself the worst thing that could happen if you don't do it. If the answer isn't too bad, then don't do it
- Anything that you can give to someone else to do.
- Anything just to please others because you fear their condemnation or you want to put them in your debt
- Thoughtless or inappropriate requests for your time and effort
- Anything others should be doing for themselves[3]

In every one-person library, there is always more than enough work to be done, and despite the advantages of good time-management practices, in order to plan and grow on the job the librarian must be able to do more – and different – things when the time comes. Calano and Salzman suggest that 'Regardless of what your field is, you must be able to manage resources. The most important of these resources is yourself.... Self-management is a career skill that will become increasingly important in the professional world as pressure for efficiency grows, stakes are raised and competition gets hotter'.[5] We would go further and suggest that in the one-person library, as management continue to demand more and more from all staff (and not just the librarian), the ability to manage time, use it effectively and efficiently, and produce services which meet the needs of the organization are not optional for the librarian: they are required.

References

1 Drucker, Peter, *The Effective Executive*. Harper and Row, New York, 1966, p. 25.

2 Berner, Andrew. 'The importance of time management in the small library,' *Special Libraries*, 78 (4), Fall 1987, p. 271.

3 LeBoeuf, Michael. *Working Smart*. Warner Books, New York, 1979, pp. 37, 103.

4 Barclay, Ian, 'Time management.' Paper delivered at the Library Association Industrial Group Annual Conference, York, March 1984.

5 Calano, Jimmy and Salzman, Jeff, 'How to get more done in a day,' *Working Woman*, April 1988, p. 99.

6 Mackenzie, Alec and Waldo, Kay Cronkite. *About Time! A Woman's Guide to Time Management*. McGraw-Hill, New York, 1981, p. 100.

7 'Concerning time management: some thoughts on interruptions.' *The One-Person Library: A Newsletter for Librarians and Management*, 3 (1), May 1986, pp.1-2.

Chapter Ten

Collection development and the acquisitions process

In the one-person library, collection development is that work which includes the formulation of and adherence to a library policy statement, the organization and development of criteria for the selection of materials for the collection, the understanding and utilization of the procedures employed in the acquisition process, and a continuous review of the collection. Each of these activities is an essential component of the librarian's management role, and none can be ignored without influencing the effective service of the one-person library.

Collection development policy

A logical starting point for a discussion of collection development, according to Andrew Berner, is to ask the question, 'What is a collection development policy and why does this library need one?'[1] According to Berner, every library has a collection development policy, although in many libraries it may exist only as informal ideas in the librarian's head. Unfortunately, this approach has two significant failings: it is very shortsighted and does not look toward the ultimate goals of the library, and as staff changes (especially in the one-person library), the informal policy is subject to change as well. Obviously, then, a written collection development policy is necessary as an aid to the librarian. No library can be all things to all people, especially in an organization or community where the library is small enough to be managed by one person. That librarian is always going to be in the position of having to pick and choose the materials to go into the collection.

What kinds of materials are collected and how does collection development begin? The American Library Association's *Guidelines for the Formulation of Collection Development* categorizes five codes or levels of collecting density: comprehensive, research, study, basic and minimal.[2] According to Susan Gensel and Audrey Powers, most special libraries, which includes most one-person libraries, collect at the research level, with timeliness the important characteristic of the collection: 'Current periodicals and online services comprise a major portion of the budget, and weeding becomes one of the most important activities in this research atmosphere'.[3] Yet there is a place for a seriously thought-out collection development policy even in those one-person libraries not in research institutions and serving a more general group of users, such as small public libraries or libraries in cultural institutions, religious organizations etc. While Gensel and Powers were addressing special libraries when they outlined their list of steps to be taken in order to begin collection development, it seems to us that all types of one-person libraries can benefit from observing the following criteria in this process:

- Understand the goal of the parent organization
- Examine the budgetary process
- Examine existing materials
- Identify all major research needs within the organization
- Determine any peripheral needs
- Establish mechanisms for selection
- Establish mechanisms for acquisitions
- Develop inventory and replacement procedures
- Prepare criteria for weeding

Berner also made a list, broader in approach, and his seven topics for consideration[1] are more applicable to the traditional one-person library, which is not so concerned with the demands for immediacy required in other libraries:

- *Acquisitions.* This involves determining the type of item which will be purchased for the collection.

- *Maintenance.* Once items are in the collection how will they be cared for on a day-to-day basis? This includes such seemingly mundane but important items as having the shelves regularly cleaned and straightened.

- *Housing and storage.* This is an adjunct of maintenance, although it deals with more long-term considerations such as temperature and humidity controls, ultraviolet filters for lights and windows etc.

- *Preservation and conservation.* This addresses the question of preserving items which are already in the collection, and includes repairing those volumes needing work, phase boxes for those beyond repair, acid-free sheets to retard deterioration, etc.

- *Replacement.* Those volumes which have been lost over the years may be replaced (in print or microform), but decisions must be made as to *which* materials will be replaced.

- *De-accessioning.* The removal of volumes which are no longer of value to the collection. This helps to solve another problem which virtually all libraries face – the lack of shelf space.

- *Gifts.* Gifts can provide a major supplement to acquisitions. However, decisions must be made as to what type of gift will be accepted, whether or not any conditions will be permitted with gifts, how they will be processed (i.e. with large gifts, is additional staff time available for processing?), how will they be acknowledged, etc.

Thus we can see that simply creating a collection development policy is a step of some importance for the one-person library, and will require serious concentration and support from management, the library committee or board, and a representative group of users.

Berner concludes his suggested directions for formulating a collection development policy with three considerations: the inclusion of the library's statement of purpose, the wording of the policy itself, and the listing of those subjects which make up the strengths of the collection. The statement of purpose, whether a memorandum from senior management creating the corporate or departmental library, or a printed document published by a town's board of managers, will list the concrete goals for the library and spell out exactly what that library is supposed to be for. The wording of the policy should be specific enough to offer guidance, but not so specific that it removes all options or initiative from the staff and governing body of the library. Finally, the policy should give indications of the specific subject areas which are of greatest significance to the library and its users, based on factors such as use and demand, the rate at which materials become dated, ease of referral to other libraries, and an analysis of the present collection. When all these are considered, the librarian and his governing board or management are in a position to create a written policy statement for the library, a statement that will be useful not only to the present librarian and management but to those who come after them.

How does the one-person librarian organize and develop criteria for the inclusion of materials in the collection? The first step, obviously, is to look at what is already there. Unless you are starting a new information service there will already be something in the library. What types of materials are there? As you look over the collection you will find that materials fall into broad categories which in an established library or information centre can include the full range of collecting instincts: books, magazines, vertical file materials (pamphlets, clippings, reports, correspondence files etc.), plus, if research is done in the parent institution, research reports, company files and similar materials (including such things as archives, photographic or other two-dimensional graphic material). Then there will be peripheral materials, often ephemeral, but items which someone at some time used in connection with his work and gave to the library when the work was finished. These include such things as consultants' reports, files relating to employees' activities in professional or trade groups, supply catalogues, and oddly enough, such ordinary things as road maps, renovation diagrams, etc. Finally, because they require special attention, some materials come to the library because of their type: one institution may store all its audiovisual materials in the library, another may keep copies of the minutes of board meetings or other institutional archives there, while a third might use the library as a storage facility for odd memorabilia: early medals, perhaps, or a couple of oil paintings, or copies of the speeches of some remote founder of the parent institution. The list can be endless, but if the one-person librarian prepares a simple inventory of the broad categories of materials in the library, he or she then has a point of departure for further consideration.

For each category of material, the library manager than asks two questions: 1) How did (does) this material get chosen for the library, and 2) Who uses it? At this point, the librarian implements the first of Echelman's responsibilities for the library manager, mentioned earlier: to establish and maintain liaison with other department and division managers, to ascertain needs and evaluate trends, and to direct the work of the library so that it meets current needs and is prepared for changes in direction before they occur.[4] In these interviews and meetings, the librarian is thus able to determine how certain categories of material are chosen and who chooses them, and to determine what materials are used and who uses them. With this information, the manager of the one-person library is now prepared to establish criteria for the inclusion or exclusion of materials in the collection. Although the librarian, management, and the library's users will all have general ideas about the goals of the parent institution, at this point it is necessary to think about how the library can *specifically* support those goals. The one-person library manager must be prepared to accept that the needs of the organization will not always be the same, and when they change, management and the librarian must be prepared to change the library's collecting policies with them. The luxury of retroactive storage is not in the purview of a collection small enough to be supervised by one person.

An additional necessary consideration for the library manager is the collecting structure in the community in which the library is located. If there are other organizations or agencies in the surrounding area which are collecting exactly what you are collecting, cooperative programmes should be investigated. Unless the one-person library is part of a parent organization in a highly competitive industry where secrecy and privileged information are required, it is to the advantage of the library and the parent institution to know what is available in other libraries and to make whatever arrangements are necessary for sharing materials.

Finally, some consideration must be given to the expertise and experience of the one-person librarian. When interviewing users and management, it is often easy to lose sight of the value of one's own training, especially if the librarian has special education in the institution's subject speciality or specialties. This background and knowledge is a valuable resource to the library, and the librarian's collecting opinions are as valid as those of users and management. In the one-person library, it may be necessary to educate users about this, but the librarian's persuasive skills can serve her well if she will use them. Her knowledge and input in the development of criteria for the inclusion of materials in the library is important to the parent organization, and her expertise must be recognized and utilized. When the librarian's knowledge of the library's subjects is combined with the thoughts and ideas of users and management and the findings of her studies of the materials already in the collection, it is possible to develop the criteria needed for collection development.

Acquisitions procedures

In the one-person library, acquisitions procedures are fairly straightforward. Once the librarian has a good understanding of the type of material he will be acquiring, he can set up routines for its selection. These will, of course, vary with the kind of library, but generally speaking materials will be chosen by the library manager based on input received from users. There may be a selection committee, made up of representative members of the user group, but even here the librarian will probably be expected to provide lists of materials and some supporting documentation such as reviews, requests from specific users for specific projects, etc. More than likely, however, the library manager will be expected to select materials based on his own research, his knowledge of the needs of the users, and his understanding of the ways in which the library supports the goals of the parent organization or community.

All of which means, of course, that the library manager must be aware of current trends in publishing in the various subjects in which the library specializes. She must know what is being published and by whom, she must read reviews and promotional materials about the subjects the library collects in, and she must, as much as possible, read some of the materials the users will be reading, particularly journals, reports and the like. This does not mean, of course, that the library manager will sit at her desk reading the library's collection of books, but it does mean that she will know her stock by title and try to find time to scan items, know the contents of books and journals coming into the library, glance over research reports, and generally do all she can to be knowledgeable about what is in the library. In the more traditional library, the library manager will, of course, rely on the catalogue, whether it is cards or computerized online, to provide a handy guide to what is in the collection. In the technical library, where the librarian is more concerned with distributing selected materials to users, she will organize a system for scanning materials in order to know what is needed and what is not. An additional consideration for the one-person librarian is that using some of one's personal time for reading is often required, simply because there is not always time to do the necessary amount of reading and study while at the office.

Collection review

It is not commonly accepted that the selection and acquisition of materials is only part of the collection development activity for a library. Now considered to be equally important is collection review – that part of library work in which materials are selected for relegation, preservation or discard (to use the terminology of the American Library Association's guidelines[2]). Most of us know this process by the less exalted but more discriptive term 'weeding,' which has unfortunate negative connotations and is, in fact, only one part of the review process. By whatever name, it is a subject which must be always at the forefront of any collection development policy in a one-person library. The ALA guidelines state:

> Most libraries are or soon will be faced by problems of change of institutional goals or programmes, space limitation, increasing collection size and cost, the impact of new programmes or needs, the problem of accumulation of duplicate or obsolescent materials which may no longer be needed in the active collection, and by the aging and decay of library materials. There is no single, or simple, answer to any of these problems, but most of them can be alleviated or reduced by a systematic, judicious, ongoing programme of collection review to identify items which may require conservation treatment, or which – for a variety of reasons – may no longer be required in the active collection. Materials review will provide better collection control, provide easier access to collections, and may achieve economies of space....[2]

Collection review should be established as part of the library's collection development policy and should be treated as a part of the library's management activity. Having established it, the librarian or his representative seeks review advice (and participation, if the library's administrative structure permits it) from the library's primary users and management to determine what materials are to be considered for discard, preservation or relegation to an off-site storage facility. It is generally not the practice in a one-person library to remove materials to a secondary collection because of shortage of space. The one-person library's collection will basically be made up of materials which are current and relevant to the work of the parent institution, and most one-person librarians will thus be dealing more with the questions of discard and preservation than with relegation. In the technical library, since most of the information dates quickly, only the most up-to-date material is retained, and the physical preservation of the collection is not a problem. It is really only in the more traditional library that preservation is a concern.

Any library must formulate criteria for weeding the collection. According to Gensel and Powers, the monograph collection must be weeded constantly, with comparisons made between new editions of older works and the discard of even slightly out-of-date material:

> There is nothing more misleading to a researcher than to discover that

an edition being used for a 'new' technique is not the latest. This should be prevented by systematic weeding.'[3]

Collection review for serial titles is a more subjective consideration, because so much of the literature used in the one-person library is in periodical or serial format. Here the librarian must think about how often a title is called for, whether it is available at a nearby library that retains a full run of the title, whether it is available under an arrangement for free exchange of photocopies between two libraries, etc. It is to the library's advantage for all arrangements to be examined before decisions are made about weeding the serials, but the primary focus must be on keeping the serials collection as current and up to date as possible, within the limitations of space and use.

There is no question but that the formulation of an appropriate collection development policy for a library is time-consuming and involved, but there can also be no question that it is necessary. It is only by creating and observing a carefully thought-out policy that the library can allocate its resources for its users in the most efficient and orderly way.

References

1 Berner, Andrew, 'Collection development,' remarks delivered at The University Club of New York, Library Associates, March 1983.

2 Perkins, David L. (ed), *Guidelines for Collection Development*, American Library Association, Collection Development Committee, Resources and Technical Services Division, Chicago, 1979, p.3.

3 Gensel, Susan and Powers, Audrey, 'Collection development and the special library,' *The New York State Library Bookmark*, 41, (1), Fall 1982, p. 11.

4 Echelman, Shirley, 'Libraries are businesses, too!' Special Libraries 65, Oct/Nov 1974, p. 410.

Chapter Eleven

Financial matters

There is a philosophical approach to librarianship which must be considered by anyone going into a one-person library. This concerns running the library in a business-like manner. We are often tempted, especially in a small library, to treat the 'behind-the-scenes' work of library administration as if it were a hobby or passing interest, but long experience has taught that the acceptance of and adherence to the practices of management and fiscal responsibility are imperative for the efficient and orderly fulfilment of the library's purpose. There is no other way of saying it: a library must be run in a business-like manner, and to treat library management in any other way is not only a disservice to users and management, it is a misuse of the funds and responsibility entrusted to the librarian.

It is useful to recognize that business management practices are required in library management, despite the fact that the 'product' is a service – the provision of information. It is a service which is difficult to quantify and often, especially in libraries which serve not-for-profit or non-profit organizations (small public libraries, church and synagogue libraries, museum libraries, etc.), difficult to justify to the laypeople who sit on committees and boards, or who are in managerial or supervisory positions in the parent organization. Nevertheless, attempts must be made to impress upon these people the businesslike makeup of the library and to encourage them to accept the fact that the library is not a cosmetic department which is tolerated and condescended to.

How do these attitudes arise among management and supervisory personnel, and even with users? How do they decide that the library is not as important as some of the other departments of the parent organization, or, indeed, as some of the other service departments? Part of the reason is a managerial reluctance to view any department that does not produce a profit as a serious part of the organization. Libraries have traditionally taken money, used it for 'running the library', a highly specialized and esoteric task as far as the layman is concerned, and at the end of the fiscal year produced no discernable profit. In these very simplistic terms, management and supervisory personnel cannot help but wonder why it costs 'so much' (no matter how little the cost!) to run a library. Never mind that the parent organization probably includes other service departments that are just as costly and provide as little – or less – return. A library, simply because so many people have preconceived notions about what one is and so little understanding of what is required to run one, is not supposed to cost anything, and when it does turn out to be expensive, much effort is required on the part of the librarian to justify the cost.

Fortunately, the attitude that libraries are no more than 'overhead' is changing, and certainly within a few years, such negative thinking will be considered dated and unproductive. Sociologically speaking, we have left the age of industry and entered an age of service. The providing of information is a service which is coming into its own; management now accepts the fact that running an organization depends on the information it has available for its decision making, and the quality of that decision making depends upon the quality of the information. Information has, it seems, become respectable.

In fact, the White House Conference on Libraries and Information Services called by President George Bush in 1991 to develop recommendations for the further improvement of the nation's library and information services and their uses by the public, was a turning point in heralding this change in attitude. The value of information, as discussed at that meeting, is directly related to productivity:

> Old definitions give way to new. Productivity, the measure of a worker's output in relation to resources, most often has been associated with raw materials and tangible resources. But a labor-intensive economic system is being supplanted by an information-based economy. That old definition now has expanded to include information as a resource, and involves reliance on judgments about source credibility, timeliness, format, and utility for application to the end product. These factors are not easily measured by traditional productivity standards, but are critical in an Information Age which can cloud a worker's sense of productive contribution to society.[1]

As attitudes change, as library and information services are looked at with 'a solid and healthy skepticism and concern',[2] the manager of a one-person library learns to recognize the importance of evaluating and justifying the library and the services it provides: these tasks form the core around which the library support is built, putting the manager of that library in a position of considerable influence in the organization. To get to that position, however, he or she must be willing to evaluate and justify the services the library provides and to master those techniques, as discussed below: evaluation and justification, despite a certain level of discomfort which they cause for some in the profession, are the foundation on which much one-person librarianship succeeds.

Nevertheless, there is another side to this picture, which has to do with size. Most one-person library managers are employed in small organizations; in these smaller companies, businesses, schools, organizations, and communities, especially those with a traditional library that provides traditional services, the impact of the information age is only just beginning to be felt. It is a fact that smaller organizations tend to take longer than larger ones to acquire new managerial methods, operational techniques, organizational approaches and, particularly, the utilization of technological innovations. The reasons are obvious: new things cost money, and if things are working all right now, there is little or no motivation for change. Not that change for its own sake is good, but when applied so that the work of the organization is done better and, more important, so that employees are rewarded and compensated beyond their salaries, change and innovation provide obvious benefits.

The need for businesslike attitudes and procedures

If we have entered an age which is accepting the cost of information as a part of doing business, how does the one-person library manager convince management and supervisory personnel that the library is a valid and reasonable place to invest resources? In addition to the evaluation and justification which emanate from the library manager himself – and which are strategically called to the attention of all management and supervisory personnel – the library is treated, literally, as if it were a small business. It is organized along businesslike lines, with appropriate record-keeping, proper accounting procedures, distinctions between tasks that are necessary and those that are not, the use of jobbers, outside agencies and other time-saving entities whenever possible and, generally, library management as if there were going to be a cash payment for the services provided. Which, in fact, there might well be, for one of the best ways to get the one-person library on to a firm, businesslike foundation is to implement a system of charging back or fees for service. According to Craig W. Wright, 'Everyone needs information, ... but providing for it in the context of maintaining a library makes it an overhead cost... by using chargebacks, a department can direct the expense of its information requests to its projects.... By rethinking the services a library provides, a more businesslike approach develops'.[3]

Charging back simply means that services or products (bibliographies, special reports etc.) emanating from the library are charged to the user's department or section. Walter E. Doherty has written about the subject, and offers handy advice in an article in which he discusses the library as a 'profit centre'.[4] Doherty defines the profit centre as 'any department, section, or part of a company, institution, or firm that brings in more money than must be paid to run it – or, at least, that brings in an amount large enough to reduce operating costs significantly'. The library can be a profit centre when management and the library manager agree that certain services can be charged back or billed to users. Doherty suggests that the list of billable services is limitless, and he begins with the library manager's time. Just as others who service the organization have billable time (lawyers, accountants etc.), so too can the librarian's time be billed back to the appropriate department or section. Time for searches is billable, as is time spent by the librarian doing in-house research. Obviously, materials and services obtained through information brokers can be charged back, and the time spent by the librarian in arranging for the job through the information broker is billed as well. In other words, anything that can be billed to a user or his or her department is charged back, with the result that a value is added to the services the library performs.

Needless to say, such programmes are not entered into without considerable thought and care. In fact, all experts on the subject of chargebacks and fees-for-service recommend determining whether such a programme is acceptable in the organization, and such determination may require considerable entrepreneurial effort on the part of the library manager. Nevertheless, the values of charging back and, where appropriate, fees for services, far outweigh the disadvantages and the effort that goes into setting them up. Simply because a tangible value is placed the services provided, chargebacks and fees are good for the library.

If the library is not part of a corporation or business but part of a non-profit or not-for-profit activity (e.g. a church, historical society, club, professional association etc.), it will present special problems, for the prevailing wisdom has not always been to treat such an institution, or its library, in a businesslike way. In 1978 William H. Newman and Harvey W. Wallender III recognized that not-for-profit enterprises were beginning to seek help from the business world in running their organizations, but they also recognized that these enterprises are different from commercial institutions.[5] Newman and Wallender described several characteristics of not-for-profit organizations, among which are several applicable to libraries, especially small ones. For one thing, service is intangible and, according to Newman and Wallender, hard to measure in such an enterprise. In the one-person library the service provided (research guidance, finding the right book or report for a user, quick-answer reference responses) is provided on a one-to-one basis between the librarian and the user. Management is seldom involved and there is no tangible way to quantify the results achieved. There are no productivity standards, no counts (except for *numbers* of books borrowed, questions answered etc., and these statistics are hardly representative of the bulk of work performed in a library, especially a one-person library), and the measurement of performance is a subjective experience on the part of those who come into the library. Newman and Wallender also point out that not only is the measurement intuitive, but the people who are judging have varying expectations.

At the same time, there are other entities which contribute to the less-than-businesslike situations so often found in not-for-profit or non-profit situations. For example, what Newman and Wallender call weak 'customer influence' comes into play, for in the one-person library the user leaves with her or her answer, book, report, journal article, or referral to another library. That user, no matter how grateful he or she might be to the librarian who helped, is highly unlikely to share that gratitude with anyone else, whether management, other users, or the man in the street.

Third, Newman and Wallender refer to something they describe as the intrusion of 'resource contributors'. In the one-person library, these are the users who stand around, read a lot and, when they have time to kill, offer advice or suggestions on library policy and procedures. Even worse, they may be board or committee members or people who make heavy financial contributions, and even though they are not qualified to manage a library, they may think they are. These people, who may be quite innocent and well meaning in their intent, can, if the librarian is not careful, become a problem when it is time to evaluate library services.

Finally, Newman and Wallender recognize charismatic leaders and/or the 'mystique' of the enterprise as constraining characteristics on effective management operations. All of us have experienced, especially in smaller organizations, the 'dynamic and forceful individual' who seems to be in charge of the enterprise. The enthusiasm is needed, and can bring many other active and useful people into the organization, but from the professional library manager's point of view it must be weighed against the work that does not get done while dealing with all the enthusiasm.

The mystique Newman and Wallender refer to can be an additional burden in a library, though conversely it can be the reason the librarian was drawn to the organization in the first place. A librarian whose personal interest or hobby embraces the subject matter of the library can have a fine time at work, but the efficient management of the library is going to be left far behind if the 'librarian' is there to use the collection for writing inspirational novels and not to care for the collection. When this mystique is coupled with the aura that surrounds libraries in general – that 'good feeling' that many laypeople have about libraries and books – the one-person librarian may very well find himself in a situation somewhat akin to working in a sanctified place. The librarian must recognize that such a situation is not really part of the professional library world and should not be passed off as such. As Newman and Wallender state: 'Once established, the mystique defines a respected role in society. The mystique sets the character and values decision makers are expected to follow'. It is easy to get too wrapped up in the ambience of one's job and forget about efficient management.

The solution to the problem is to be found in the person who has the job of running the library:

> ...the critical task is integration. The interests and values of contributors may differ sharply from those of scientists, prima donnas and doctors who actually create the services of the enterprise... A special need arises for people in buffer roles, who can relate to both inside and outside groups and can promote agreement on actions to be taken. This integrating task is especially difficult in enterprises where the service is intangible and the objectives are multiple and shifting.[5]

In the one-person library, the library manager can be the integrator, if he or she is willing to take up the challenge. In fact, the library manager has a splendid opportunity to take on a strong leadership role in the organization or institution, for he or she can question the assumption that the service is intangible. There are those who are doing so, and their work is providing the profession with new directions in the measurement of services. W. David Penniman, for example, has suggested that a new philosophy of information services leadership is possible, and necessary, as the profession plans for the future:

> I would argue that we must change the way we measure success for our information service providers.... The traditional view is that information organizations are institutions providing service of immeasurable value. Most libraries function under this philosophy. ... As the overhead costs of information services in all institutions come under the magnifying glass, this philosophy, I am convinced, will cease to be viable.
>
> The alternative philosophy is that every information service/product has a measurable value. The value of a service may be its cost versus the cost of a competing service when the unit costs of both are made explicit. However value is computed, it needs to be made explicit, or the value will end up being realized too late as the lost opportunity cost once the service is eliminated.
>
> In the immeasurable value approach, information services are justified on qualitative assertions. Resources required are quantified (i.e. budgets), but output measures are de-emphasized (instead, 'value' is measured by volumes held or size of budget). The link between mission and output is subjective and productivity is not (and cannot be) measured. Budgets grow or shrink incrementally (e.g. cut budget by 10%), and accountability focuses on resources used. Consequently, costs are almost always viewed as something to be reduced, since they are not directly linked to benefits.
>
> In the second, measured-value approach, organizations are justified by quantitative assertions (i.e. improved reference service productivity by 20%, provided a return-on-investment of 35%, decreased cataloguing expenses by 20% while holding output constant). Resources required are quantified but so is output, and productivity is measured. The link between mission and output is objective, and budgets can take into account individual programme benefits so that decisions can be made on the basis of strategic payoffs. Accountability focuses on output as well as input measures.[7]

Evaluation and justification

How does the manager of a one-person library focus on 'output as well as input' measures? There is a variety of ways, but one of the best is to look at return on investment. The process for libraries and information centres was outlined by Helen M. Manning in a paper delivered in 1989. Although designed for a large installation, the process is applicable to even the smallest one-person library, for the survey instrument asked basic questions which every library manager needs to have answered. For example, a list of services was offered, with respondents ranking the value of each service. Additionally, questions were asked about the level of usage during a given time frame, and workers were asked to determine the impact library services had on their ability to do their work (with suggested responses ranging from 'No impact' to 'significant impact', with a category for 'don't know' included as well). Finally, each respondent was asked how many hours library services saved him or her per month, and how many hours the librarian saves him or her per month. The analysis of the survey results in this case determined that the return on investment in one of the participating libraries was 515%. During the year being analysed, library operations and personnel saved the company $959,000, yet the same services cost only $186,000. Using these same methods, other libraries in the organization produced similarly spectacular returns, with the average being about 400%.[7]

Doris Johnson at Northeast Utilities in Hartford, Connecticut, took a slightly different approach.[8] Her idea was to put herself on the other side of the survey, since she knew that busy engineers and technicians had tight schedules and might not take the time to complete a full survey, so simplicity of response and time for response was of primary value to her. Johnson's six survey questions were designed specifically for estimating the value of the one-person operation:

1. How many times per year do you use the Research Information Centre?

2. Have you used the online searching service?

3. If yes, were the results satisfactory?

4. How would you rate the results?
    Adequate
    More than adequate
    Less than adequate
    Other

5. If you did not have this search service, would you have pursued outside sources (such as public libraries, industry libraries, etc.) to obtain the information?

    If yes, where?

6. How many hours per year do you estimate the Research Information centre's services have saved you, as opposed to your searching outside the company for information?

    1 – 10
    11 – 20
    21 – 30
    More? How many?

The survey was not sent to everyone, and in fact Johnson chose those engineers and technicians who were more active users, for she was not trying to estimate the value of the information centre for the company as a whole (although that became a goal later on) but rather to determine how its services were of use to its users. The results for Johnson were positive, with some departments reporting savings of 320 – 340 hours during a year. Multiplying these figures by the average hourly salary of the users gave Johnson solid, useful information for proving the value of her operation to the company. It is an approach that any one-person library manager can adopt, and the resulting information, in measurable terms (that management personnel understand) and not in vague intangibles, is a useful way of describing the value of the library or information centre to the parent organization, a point that Penniman made:

> This second mechanism [the measured value approach] has serious implications for the infrastructure of an organization. It moves that organization and its services into the mainstream of the broader community in which it resides. It positions the library, for example, as a delivery mechanism rather than a warehouse, with an emphasis on output, not assets.[6]

The budgeting process

Sylvia Webb poses a fundamental question that must be answered before we can begin to define budgets and describe the budgeting procedure: 'Was or is there a separate budget; who has overall responsibility for it?'[9] In the one-person library the librarian must determine who provides funding for the library and whether the librarian is to have input into the funding decisions.

   If the library is part of a corporate parent organization, funding decisions may very well not be made with the librarian's advice. If this is the case, she should early on begin submitting financial estimates, keeping appropriate account books (even if unaudited) and performing similar budgeting procedures as if she were in charge of the budget, in order to ensure that her managers and supervisors recognize that she understands the budget process. In other words, the librarian must act as if she is part of the budget process even when she is not. It is part of the businesslike management of the library, and it will enable her, at the appropriate time, to request and assume full financial responsibility for the information service for which she has all other responsibility.

   On the other hand, in a small public library or the library of a historical society or art museum, the librarian may be the only person who is in a position to know how much is to be spent in the library. In either case, it is important for the librarian to know how much influence he or she has in the budget procedure, and to plan how to use that influence to the best advantage.

Budgets are defined in different ways, and many library management experts have tried to come up with a workable definition. Evans, in *Management Techniques for Librarians*, says that budgets are:

> ...simply plans of action expressed in terms of cost. These costs may be dollars or man-hours, or machine-hours, or some combination of these factors. They do not have to be stated in dollars and cents. Budgets are estimates of what management thinks it will cost to carry out a plan of operation for the organization during a specified period of time.[10]

Sinclair, on the other hand, speaking of small public libraries, puts the emphasis not on the plan of operation but on the cooperation between the librarian and the board:

> The most important part of library business in which the librarian and board work together is the preparation of the budget. A budget, like much else in library management, is made easier by careful planning. The year's budget might be considered a programme for the coming year's activities with price tags attached to the various items. If librarian and trustees are agreed on objectives and have worked out together a long-range plan for library development, preparation of a budget becomes a matter of determining how much of the programme can be attempted in any particular year in light of current costs and local financial conditions. If the long-range plan has been approved in principle by the appropriating or taxing body or by planning officials, as well as by the library board, preparing the budget and securing approval become even simpler.[11]

Blagden, writing on financial management in Aslib's *Handbook of Special Librarianship and Information Work*, defines a budget as:

> ...the mechanism by which funds are granted... In putting forward proposals for funding it is, of course, important to spell out the overall role of the library and information service in supporting the goals of the host organization, and to specify in some detail exactly how this role will be translated into practice.[12]

When we turn from strictly library considerations we find that the definitions and procedures are not much different. Gross and Warshauer, accountants writing for non-profit organizations, offer these basic steps:

1. A list of objectives or goals of the organization for the following year should be prepared. For many organizations this process will be essentially a re-evaluation of the relative priority of the existing programmes. Care should be taken, however, to avoid concluding too hastily that an existing programme should continue unchanged. Our society is not static and the organization that does not constantly re-evaluate and update its programmes is in danger of being left behind.

2. The cost of each objective or goal listed above should be estimated. For continuing programmes, last year's actual expense and last year's budget will be the starting point. For new programmes or modifications of existing programmes, a substantial amount of work may be necessary to accurately estimate the costs involved. This estimating process should be done in detail since elements of a particular goal or objective may involve many categories of expenses or salaries.

3. The expected income of an organization should be estimated... Organizations are often overly optimistic in estimating income. This can prove to be the organization's downfall if there is no margin for error, and realism must be used or the budget will have little meaning.

4. The total expected income should be compared to the expense of achieving the objectives or goals.

5. The final proposed budget should be submitted to the appropriate body for ratification... This should not be just a formality but should be carefully presented to the ratifying body so that, once ratified, all persons will be firmly committed to the resulting plan of action.[13]

As Gross and Warshauer emphasize, these steps may seem so elementary that to repeat them is probably unnecessary, but experience shows that many one-person librarians do not give the budget process the time and consideration it requires. It is not a matter of choice: either the steps are taken or the library budget is not properly prepared.

The obvious theme running through these definitions, as well as in all other approaches to budgeting procedures, is the concept of planning. We begin by going back to basics: What is my library supposed to be doing? According to Murray S. Martin, who edited *Financial Planning for Libraries*, libraries must 'return to their basic role – the collection and organization of information'.[16] This requires that each one-person librarian plan his budget in terms of the library's role in the parent institution, how it is expected to perform that role and how much it costs to do so. If we are doing things in the library that are not part of that role, we need to stop and question if they should be paid for from library funds. Martin then suggests that we reassess the role of libraries within the professional world, recognizing that the publishing world is changing (and with it the library world), so part of our request for materials must include funding for non-traditional expenditures such as increased interlibrary loans, online services, free or inexpensive copying facilities, facsimile services, contracted services, etc. Finally, we must place our money 'where it is most needed'. This means that we must first fund the essential services and programmes, and question any that are marginal, even if they are our favourites.

In Martin's book on the subject, Harold R. Jenkins has written a piece advocating an 'umbrella' concept for public libraries that can be applied to one-person library operations. Jenkins is an optimist, who takes a positive attitude to budgeting, and suggests an approach which 'covers planning, controlling, organizing and detailing each projected step of a contemplated action leading to a specific objective. Obviously budgeting should not be seen as an unwelcome constraint but rather as a welcomed opportunity to see one's way into the future'.[15]

Can such an optimistic approach work in the one-person library? Yes, if the librarian is willing to take planning and budgeting work seriously. It is not easy, especially in organizations where the library is considered unimportant by management and supervisory personnel, but if the librarian is willing to take on the extra challenge of proving that the library is a serious part of the organization, educating and stimulating people to see the library this way, the extra time and effort will not have been wasted.

Various types of budgets are recognized for library work. The most commonly accepted is the line or formula budget, which, as Evans[10] points out, usually means operating expenses, although the line budget also includes capital expense or capital outlay. The operating expense usually covers such items as books and materials, salaries, utilities, maintenance, supplies, travel and insurance.

Other types of budgets include the performance budget, which Evans describes as 'based on functions, activities, and projects... a financial plan prepared, analysed and interpreted in terms of the services and activities themselves', and which he applies to library work by pointing out that the

> ...ultimate objective of a library is to provide service. The library's profit is thought of in terms of the degree to which its services are used and the satisfaction derived by the patron. Thus, the budget, which explains expenditures in terms of accomplishments and results rather than strictly in terms of objects, can be very useful because it is oriented toward the real goals of the library'[10]

Performance budgeting, while beneficial in many respects, does present some problems. According to Blagden in the *Aslib Handbook*, there are two: the performance budget 'can be a very time-consuming exercise and some of the decisions regarding the allocation of costs to different services will be done on a somewhat arbitrary basis'.[12] Thus we have a classic conflict for the one-person librarian, who would like to use the budgeting procedure which would most accurately reflect the work being done in the library but, unfortunately, is limited by the very same restrictions which Blagden describes.

There have been attempts to determine just how much it should cost an organization to support a library. Ashworth suggests the following:

> The cost of running a special library is a matter of extreme variability in practice. Managements should not think of allocating less than one fiftieth of their total research budget to the library; and for the fullest service, covering every type of information dissemination, at least one-thirtieth to one-twentieth should be the aim. The latter figure would be for smaller organizations, as there is a minimum size of library

which would be viable to support an innovative team. For this a moderate collection of textbooks (say 5000 volumes), a small intensively selected reference stock (200 volumes), and at least 200 current periodicals, amongst which would be sets of relevant abstract journals, would be essential stock. This would be supported by pamphlets, patents, reports, standard specifications etc., as appropriate. Such a library could be maintained by one person, though the addition of more staff would be highly desirable – and essential as soon as the library increased appreciably beyond the minimum size.[16]

There are a few basic tips for the librarian who is contemplating the annual budget proposal. After reading all the appropriate literature on the subject and consulting with users and supervisors, the one-person library manager should give some thought to the following:

1. Question everything. Before your supervisor or manager asks why something is in the budget, be sure you can justify it yourself (and if you think it can be deleted from the budget, suggest deleting it – do not include it just because 'it has always been there'). Be ruthless.

2. Be realistic and be attuned to what is going on in the parent institution or the community. If profits or income are down, do not ask for funding for a marginal item.

3. On the other hand, do not restrict your planning to available income. If the item is important enough, and if you do a proper job of recognizing and reporting its need, management just might find the money for it.

4. Be businesslike. We must employ the same procedures regarding hours of service, staff involvement, purchasing, user relations and cost-effectiveness that we would employ if our users were purchasing – for an established price – the services we give them free (after all, somebody is paying for these services; the difference is that we do not see the money directly).

5. Keep it simple. Try to eliminate the layers. If we simply think of budgeting as using our available funds to best advantage we can cut through a lot of the rhetoric.

6. Look for substitutes. If there is a cheaper way of doing something, try it. Leasing equipment, for example, can be cheaper in the long run because you are not trying to obtain service or parts for obsolete machinery. Similarly, using a periodicals subscription agency, even for a small list, saves time. Look for short cuts.

7. Proselytize. Be political. There is nothing secret about the budget (or there shouldn't be), so if you need to speak to someone about it, go ahead. If there is a user who can be helpful, seek his help. Management might well approve a microfilm reader–printer if the users have made it clear that they need one. Have some of them write letters or make tele-

phone calls. Your library can use its supporters. If people write fan letters to you, write back and ask them if they would be willing to help you seek additional funding for the library.

8. Finally: read; listen; learn. If you know a manager (or another librarian) who is especially skilled in budget work, get to know him or her better to learn what contributes to that department's success. Look for budget articles in the professional media. If you don't have extensive accounting background, seek out books like G. Stevenson Smith's *Accounting for Librarians and Other Not-for-Profit Managers*.[17] Another useful title is the previously cited *Financial and Accounting Guide for Nonprofit Organizations*, by Malvern J. Gross, Jr. and William Warshauer, Jr.[13] Also, *The Bottom Line Reader: A Financial Handbook for Librarians*[18] would be a useful investment.

The budgeting procedure does not have to be a negative experience, an annual chore anticipated with anxiety. For the one-person librarian, in addition to being an opportunity to plan for the year ahead, the budget review is also an opportunity to promote a positive relationship with management and supervisory personnel. These people can be educated to recognize that the library is a serious and responsible part of the parent organization, and at the same time, be made aware of how the one-person library manager anticipates what is to be achieved in the next budget period.

References

1   *Information 2000–Library and Information Services for the 21st Century: Summary Report of the 1991 White House Conference on Library and Information Services*, Washington DC, 1991, p. 5.

2   St. Clair, Guy. 'Thinking about... WHCLIS and the one-person library,' *The One-Person Library: A Newsletter for Librarians and Management*, 8, (4), August 1991, p.7.

3   Wright, Craig E., 'The corporate information challenge: streamlining external information,' *Records Management Quarterly*, 25, (3), July 1991, pp. 14–16.

4   Doherty, Walter E. , 'How to turn a library into a profit centre: the law library example,' In: *The Bottom Line Reader: A Financial Handbook for Librarians*. Neal- Schuman, New York, 1990, pp. 141–142.

5   Newman, William H. and Wallender, Harvey W., 'Managing not-for-profit enterprises,' *Academy of Management Review*, 3, (1), 1978, 24–31.

6. Penniman, W. David, *Preparing for Future Information Delivery Systems*, the Second Annual John T. Corrigan Memorial Lecture, 3 May 1991, Washington DC: The Council of National Library and Information Associations, CNLIA Occasional Paper No. 2, pp. 7–8.

7 Manning, Helen M., 'The corporate librarian: great return on investment,' In: *Information: A Strategy for Economic Growth*, Papers presented at the State-of-the-Art Institute, November 6–8, 1989, Washington DC (Washington DC, Special Libraries Association, 1990) pp. 7–17.

8 Johnson, Doris E., 'The information centre: necessity or luxury?' *The One-Person Library: A Newsletter for Librarians and Management*, 4, (1), May, 1987, pp. 1–3.

9 Webb, Sylvia, *Creating an Information Service*, Aslib, London, 1983, p.10.

10 Evans, G. Edward, *Management Techniques for Librarians*. Academic Press, New York, 1976, p. 100.

11 Sinclair, Dorothy, *The Administration of the Small Public Library*, American Library Association, Chicago, 1979, p. 60.

12 Blagden, J., 'Financial management,' In: Anthony, L.J. (ed), *Handbook of Special Librarianship and Information Work*. Aslib, London, 1982, p. 55.

13 Gross, Malvern J. and Warshauer, William, Jr. *Financial and Accounting Guide for Nonprofit Organizations*. John Wiley and Sons, New York, 1979, pp. 316–317.

14 Martin, Murray S. (ed), *Financial Planning for Librarians*. The Haworth Press, New York, 1983, p. 4.

15 Jenkins, Harold S., 'Returning to the unified theory of budgeting: an umbrella concept for public libraries,' In: Martin, *op.cit.*, p. 75.

16 Ashworth, Wilfred, *Special Librarianship*. Outlines of Modern Librarianship. Clive Bingley, London, 1979.

17 Smith, Stevenson G. *Accounting for Librarians and Other Not-for-Profit Managers*, American Library Association, Chicago, 1983.

18 Sellen, Betty-Carol and Turock, Betty J., (eds), *The Bottom Line Reader: A Financial Handbook for Librarians*. Neal-Schuman, New York, 1990.

Chapter Twelve

Information technology in the one-person library

In 1986, the one-person library manager thought about information technology in terms of feasibility. In the new one-person library, this is not even an issue: information technology is here to stay. It is part of the library and information services profession, and the manager of a one-person library or information centre not only uses it to provide a better service for his users, but information technology provides the very means by which is able to do his work.

The concept was neatly summarized by Cheryl Pfeifer in a paper delivered in 1990. Pfeifer noted that:

> A new generation of users is coming into our special libraries today. They are familiar with the many innovations in information technology. With the availability of CD-ROM systems, online searches, after-hours services, menu-driven files, 24 hour access to online catalogs, end-user software, and the increasing use of full-text databases, these are knowledgeable and sophisticated users … demanding more expertise from us as information professionals....

> Library automation in the last 10–20 years has dramatically changed the way we locate and access information. What we thought were the implications of technology then are different than what transpired. New information technologies have pushed us into the third generation of automation. The first generation automated the basic functions of a library. It provided us with online access to our catalogs, and a means of doing a computerized literature search of indexes currently in print. The second generation has allowed us to order documents online, to actually search and view documents online, to search indexes that aren't in any other form except online, and provided remote access to our collections. We are well into the third generation of automation now... We have coped and accepted technology with open arms to get rid of some of the drudgery and make our positions more exciting. Technology has not gotten the best of us. We have met the challenge....[1]

The challenge for the manager of the one-person library is to determine which technology to use. To all intents and purposes the choices are limitless, and the services the one-person library is able to provide are limited only by the service and support parameters agreed upon by the librarian and his or her managers. At the very least, the one-person library will have a telephone, preferably with facsimile capabilities, a personal computer with wordprocessing, database and basic accounting software, and a good quality photocopier. The next level of service will incorporate search capability, including the addition of a modem to the personal computer, and the consideration of a local area network so that the one-person library is connected with the computers of others in the parent organization.

Services to users, and the level of information technology to support those services, will be determined in conversations with management and users, as discussed earlier. Undoubtedly (unless the library is part of an organization in which management has made a conscious decision not to offer search services), this will be a major activity. Database searching is a basic component in library and information work today, a finding borne out in a study of management views of library services, which determined that some 80% of their survey group cite database searching as a key service.[2].

However database searching is one part of the picture. In 1989, a survey of American and Canadian special librarians (of which one-person librarians made up 13.7% of the 4036 respondents) determined that technology was an important part of their professional lives.[3] In fact, only 1.9% of the respondents indicated that none of the applications or tools listed in the survey were used in their libraries and information centres. As a checklist of what can be done with information technology, the tools and applications listed in the survey and available for one-person libraries and information centres are as follows:

- word processing
- online external databases
- online internal databases
- telecommunications
- spreadsheet
- electronic mail and messaging
- optical scanners
- optical digital disks
- facsimile communications
- database management
- database administration
- computer-based training
- CD-ROM

- shared cataloging systems

- desktop publishing

- automated interlibrary loans

- serials routing

- automated acquisitions system

- automated circulation system

- current awareness

- abstracting and indexing system

- automated thesaurus construction

Any and all of these services will be considered by the one-person library manager as she and her managers work together to determine what the information needs of the organization are, and how the library will service those needs.

Automated library functions

To determine which services are to be automated and which left as manual, the manager of the one-person library must engage in a series of planning discussions. He will recognize that there is a place in the library operation for the computer-based or automated library function – defined by John Corbin as a function in which the 'computer is used to support a library function—that is, when a computer performs some of the basic processing operations in a function such as acquiring, cataloging, and circulating materials; or providing access to information'.[4] He recognizes, similarly, that the computer and the librarian will, 'share responsibility' for carrying out work, as the computer will manipulate or act upon information keyed into the system in order to trigger the sought-after response. Effective information technology, particularly automation, is a partnership in which the staff member and the machine work together to arrive at a useful result.

In considering which tasks to automate, the best advice was given several years ago by Katherine Kyes Leab. In a talk entitled 'The Computer in the One-Person Library: Useful Tool or Killer Toy?' Leab's advise was basic: you read all you can, and you prepare a list of what you do.

> You must think about the procedures you follow in your library, and you must consider them as precisely as you possibly can. You must write them down, study them, and understand exactly why you practise each of them. Why? Because a small library is like a small business, and you must thoroughly do your groundwork... After you've read all you can and analyzed your procedures to your satisfaction, give some thought to the most efficient manual system or procedure that you use. Then ask

yourself the basic question: Will computerizing that procedure save the library time and money? If not, then you might be wise to decide against computerizing.[5]

What most one-person library managers discover, of course, is that automating the procedure will indeed save time and money, and it is then up to the librarian to determine which automated procedure is best for his or her particular situation.

Information sources

Leab's admonition to read is not lost on the one-person librarian, but the problem is not so much choosing to read as choosing what to read. The literature of information technology is almost overwhelming in its variety and scope, and without a doubt, beyond the capacity of any library manager. One must therefore seek short-cuts, but, in taking the time to find out what is available, one is also learning about the technology and how it might be of value in the one-person library.

The first place the library manager looks is to the literature, of course, and there are many titles which, when browsed through, will offer guidelines about information technology. The regular columns in the standard professional journals are a good, solid source of information, and the popular material on automation can provide much guidance. As discussed earlier, networking with other librarians is exceptionally valuable, and this is where those memberships of professional associations and local networking groups have their primary value. The smart one-person library manager will take advantage of every opportunity to attend continuing education courses, informal or more formal lunch meetings, and similar gatherings where librarians share information. Colleagues can often provide the best guidance for the one-person library manager who is thinking about installing a new product or service, and even if the decision is made not to go ahead the exchange with other library managers can be beneficial. Another source is on-site, for within the organization or community, the people who work in electronic data processing already know what systems can work best with what is already in place, and can be a valuable resource for information.

Vendors

Conference programmes and vendor exhibits where products and services are displayed are a major source of useful information for the one-person library manager. Vendors have a wealth of knowledge to impart to librarians who are interested in their products, and there are ways to take advantage of their expertise. A list of these appeared in an early issue of *The One-Person Library*,[6] and the guidelines are still valuable. Although the subject of the article was the purchase of any sort of major equipment or appliance for the one-person library, the advice is especially appropriate for library managers considering an investment in new or different forms of information technology:

- Use sales people as a resource: There is only so much that you can learn from brochures and catalogues. You are going to want specific answers to specific questions, and only a sales person can be helpful, so allow him or her to be.

- Do not create an adversary relationship. Of course the sales person wants to make a sale, but he also wants to be helpful, so allow him to.

- Make an appointment. If a sales person just drops in or if you receive a telephone solicitation (and it is a product you are interested in) tell her that you are too busy to talk, but you will be glad to make an appointment for a future meeting. This will give you a chance to collect your thoughts.

- See sales people at your office, at the library or information centre where you work. If the meeting takes place on your 'turf' you will be more comfortable. If the product requires a demonstration, see if it can be done at the library. If not, you should still have your initial meeting at the library and arrange for a later demonstration at the showroom.

- Be prepared. Before the sales person calls, you should know something about the product. Have a list of specific questions written down and leave space between them to jot down the responses.

- Do not be afraid of appearing foolish. If you have a question, ask it. If you do not understand the response, say so. You are not expected to know everything about every product in advance.

- Do not worry about wasting the sales person's time. He gets paid for it. Take as long as you feel you need. If the sales person seems to be rushing you it is a clear sign that you should look elsewhere. On the other hand, do not feel that you have to buy something because the sales person has been pleasant and has spent a lot of time with you. If he does not make a sale, he loses a commission, but if you buy something you do not really want or need, you are stuck with it.

- Ask for the names and telephone numbers of other people in the area (especially librarians and other information services professionals) who have purchased or use the product. Contact them to find out if they are satisfied. Also find out if they have had any problems obtaining service for the product, if this is required.

- Do not be afraid to talk about money. It is, after all, a major factor in your decision.

- If you are considering a large purchase, look into financing. You will pay more in the long run but you will not be putting a great strain on your budget at any one time. But be sure to check the interest rates, and back away from any that seem unreasonable to you.

- If the sales person tells you that her product does not currently meet all your requirements but that her company is working on 'add-ons' that will be ready in a few months, politely (or not so politely) show her the door.

- If you are really interested in a product and it is a big-ticket item, ask the sales person to prepare a formal proposal tailored to your specific needs. If you feel more comfortable, tell him that you need it for your committee or management. Sales people are always anxious to impress important decision makers in the organization.

- If you mean 'no', say 'no'. This is one of the hardest things to do since it means 'insulting' the sales person, but it is better to do this than to waste her time as she comes for additional sales calls or prepares proposals if you have already made up your mind that you are not interested.

- If you feel that the sales person is not being honest, or if you feel that he is trying to pressure you, find another product. The product should sell itself. You should have a feeling of confidence that it meets your needs. The sales person should spend more time answering your questions than 'selling'.

- You may not have to buy the product at all. Ask the sales person about leasing. With many products the state of the art changes so rapidly that a product may be obsolete within a few years. Leasing allows you to keep up with changes in technology without having to unload obsolete equipment.

Dealing with the end user

In the one-person library community, there continues to be considerable discussion about the role of the librarian and the role of the end user, particularly in terms of automation and information technology. There is the question of who is better qualified to search, the librarian or the end user. In many situations, the librarian has been trained in search skills, understands the organization of information, and is the expert when it comes to database searching. Yet users in the company or institution, intrigued by the possibility of cutting out the go-between – the librarian – ask for and receive basic training so that they can do their own searching.

For many one-person librarians, end-user searching is seen as something of a threat, for they rightly regard their search skills as but one part of the information delivery package they provide. Some end users succeed very well with their searching. In hospital libraries, for example, 'The physician, the main user of the hospital library, is becoming very computer literate and in many cases is performing his/her own MEDLINEs. Value issues and cost issues seem to matter little – the physician likes performing searches whether they are done well or not'.[7]

Yet there is another side to the story. For many of those end users who do their own searching, there often comes a moment of awakening, a time when they realize that the product of their searches is not as useful or as thorough as they need it to be, and they find themselves going to the librarian for further guidance. Or, as is often the case, because they are not interested in learning beyond the basic search skills, they lose interest and to obtain a complete result, they must come back to the librarian. In either scenario, the librarian regains the role she feared she had lost, for she is, indeed, the information 'counsellor' who can provide users with the level of information retrieval and delivery that they themselves cannot provide.

Nevertheless, there are programmes and systems which are designed for end-users, and when these are installed in an organization and some of the searching is taken away from the one-person librarian, it is not necessarily a time to panic. Database searching is but one of several important services the library offers, and for the manager of a one-person operation, whose time is already stretched, the loss of some of the searching may, in fact, be a positive step, since it allows time for other professional tasks which might otherwise be neglected.

The subject of end-user searching continues to receive attention in the profession, and it was addressed by Matarazzo, Prusak and Gauthier:[2]

> The increased importance of databases presents some potential problems for librarians because it leads to increased pressure for end-user searching. Vendors promote the end-user-initiated search for commercial reasons; end users, especially those with computer knowledge, often see no need for an intermediary to do the searches. In some fast-paced environments, the user of a librarian can be viewed as a hindrance – a gatekeeper who adds little value in the database search.

> The practice of letting end-user searching occur has proved on occasion to be quite expensive to firms, due to seriously inexperienced and ill-trained searchers. In several cases, the firms eliminated the practice and went back to giving the library the monopoly on database searching. However, more frequent and better training by vendors, consultants and librarians may make this practice more viable.

Whatever the final outcome, it is clear that in the area of end-user searching, the role the librarian plays, whether it is as searcher, trainer or information counsellor, is one that will continue to be viable for a long time to come.

Enhancing the value of the library/information centre.

Finally, any consideration of automation and information technology must include some recognition of the fact that, in today's society, automated services go a long way toward changing perceptions of management and users about the value of the library. Librarians are frequently being admonished to speak to management in management terms; nothing conveys the traditional, 'bookish' image of librarianship better than a library which has not automated when all other sections of an organization are using information technology. Gary Lance wrote forcefully about this when he was advising librarians in news bureaux and the media: 'Automate the library – give management the facts and figures; show them you know the technology. Get management involved with a library automation committee. No other single project has given the library greater visibility in the last few years....'[8]

The fact of the matter is that management and users are served by information technology in all other aspects of their personal and professional lives, so it makes sense that the same technology should be applied to their information needs. It is no longer a matter of choice, for information technology enables the library to provide the services its users need, and without it, one-person librarians are relegated to a less-than-necessary role in the organization.

References

1 Pfeifer, Cheryl, 'Redefining the role of the information specialist n response to technology,' In: *The Information Professional: An Unparalleled Resource*, Papers Contributed for the 81st Annual Conference of the Special Libraries Association, June 9-14 1990, Pittsburgh, PA. Washington DC: Special Libraries Association, 1991, pp. 71-74.

2 Matarazzo, James M., Prusak, Laurence, and Gauthier, Michael R., *Valuing Corporate Libraries: A Survey of Senior Managers*, Special Libraries Association, Washington DC, 1990. p.7.

3 Brimsek, Tobi A, *Powering Up: A Technological Assessment of the SLA Membership*, Special Libraries Association, Washington, DC, 1990, pp. iii.

4 Corbin, John, *Implementing the Automated Library System*, Oryx, Phoenix, AZ, 1988, p. 1.

5 Leab, Katherine Kyes, 'The new communications: variety and impact – part one,' *The One-Person Library: A Newsletter for Librarians and Management*, 2, (4), August 1985, pp. 4-5.

6 'When a salesman comes to call', *The One-Person Library: A Newsletter for Librarians and Management,* 1, (8), December 1984, pp. 2-3.

7 Hull, Nina N., 'Hospital OPLs face the 90s,' *The One-Person Library: A Newsletter for Librarians and Management,* 7, (6), October 1990, pp. 3-5.

8 Lance, Gary, 'Improve your library's image,' *News Libraries News,* 11, (1), Fall 1988, pp. 3-4.

Chapter Thirteen

Marketing the one-person library

In the last years of the 20 century, much attention is being given to the concept that library and information services cannot be reactive, but rather must be *proactive*, and today's professional is expected to go to users and convince them that it is to their benefit to make use of the services. A proactive one-person library manager does not wait for the users to come to the library – the library manager goes to the users.

This, in effect, is the thrust behind the marketing programme for the one-person library. The librarian knows that the services she offers have been designed to serve the mission of the supporting organization. The librarian knows the value of the service, and she recognizes that the more it is used, the more successful the organization will be in achieving its mission. Therefore, she takes it upon herself to market library and information services. She becomes, for her users, an entrepreneur within the organization.

The librarian as entrepreneur

Despite the fact that entrepreneurship is generally associated with selling a product or service to the public, there is definitely a place for entrepreneurial values in librarianship. The characteristics of these values have been variously defined, but for the one-person library world, they would seem to fall into certain distinct patterns, as identified by Gifford Pinchot in another context. Entrepreneurs, it seems, are people who have a deep need for achievement, who take calculated, moderate risks, who use analytical skills in their work, and who insist on honesty and integrity in their work.[1] They are also, we would submit, people who have a vision of their organization or community that drives them to share in the achievement of the organizational mission.

Pinchot argued that these people (whom he called 'intrapreneurs'), if they are permitted to stay within an organization and do not go off on their own, can make a valuable contribution to that organization. Herbert White argued just as persuasively that these people are absolutely essential to library and information services organizations. In fact, in White's words, '...probably no profession has a greater need for this newly termed intrapreneur than librarianship'.[2]

Such entrepreneurial spirit is, of course, the primary ingredient in the one-person library's marketing programme, for before he sells anything else, the librarian is selling himself and the quality of the service provided. That service must be client- or user-oriented, and it must reflect the needs of the defined user base, as determined through interviews, questionnaires and other techniques the librarian will employ. Other characteristics of quality service, as identified by Meg Paul,[3] include:

- accurate and reliable information

- seriousness about the high level of service

- no wrong answers

- accessibility, approachability

- hard work

- staff satisfaction with results

- the client is always right

If the one-person library offers a quality service, and the manager of the library has (or can adopt) an entrepreneurial attitude the work, marketing the service can proceed with relative ease.

Promotion, public relations and marketing

The terms are not interchangeable, although they are frequently confused. Public relations is defined as an attempt 'to influence public opinion by conveying information that benefits the [library] through a variety of techniques that will result in favorable publicity...'[4] Marketing, on the other hand, has a variety of definitions, but Lawraine Wood, from Loughborough University's Centre for Library and Information Management, provides the best version: 'Marketing is a planned approach to identifying, attracting, serving and gaining support of the specific user groups in a manner that furthers the goals of the library and the organization which it supports.'[5] Promotion seems to combine the two. The dictionary definition calls it the 'active furtherance or sale of merchandise through advertising or other publicity', and offers 'publicity' as a synonym. Helen M. Gothbert, writing in *Library Administration and Management*, says of promotion that it 'is not, in and of itself, public relations; it is a tool of public relations'.[6]

Marketing for libraries is further defined by Philip A. Kotler: 'The term *marketing* refers to the effective management by an organization of its exchange relations with its various publics',[7] and Joyce A. Edinger builds on this: 'The obvious reason for librarians to become involved in a formalized effort of this nature is to improve the satisfaction of the potential library patron..." Edinger takes Kotler's 'marketing concept' (which calls for a basic reorientation of the organization from looking inward toward its products and services to looking outward toward the consumer's needs) and applies it to libraries in an exercise that has obvious benefits for the one-person library: 'the patron is the focus instead of the librarian, and the patron is the librarian's reason for being'.[8]

The benefits of an effective marketing programme

There are four benefits in marketing the one-person library, all of which have been discussed variously elsewhere but which bear repeating here. Marketing increases the use of the library or information centre, enabling the manager of the one-person library to add new clients to the defined user base. Marketing adds to the value of the library or information centre in the organization or community, especially in terms of what its services can provide for potential users who have not previously been aware of the library and is programmes. Marketing is used for the education of users and non-users alike. Users become aware of new or different services which can aid them in their work, and even those people who do not have occasion to use the library become part of the marketing effort, as they tell other people about what the library offers. Finally, marketing brings about changed perceptions, for the library which is marketed throughout the organization or community is thereby perceived as contributing to the organizational mission.

Several specific areas should be addressed by the one-person librarian as he or she begins to implement a marketing plan. As outlined by St. Clair in 1990,[9] these are:

1. How does money come into the organization or community? You need to know who controls it, how it is spent, and where it is allocated within the organization. If there is a department that seems always to be adequately funded, you need to look at that department and see what services and programmes it is offering. How essential are they? Is the library/information service analogous in any way with what is being done in that department? As for the staff that control the money, how well versed are those people about the services and value of the library to the organization? Even if they don't use the library at all, they can be made aware of what the library does.

2. How does the library or information service contribute to the organization's goals and successes? If the organization is a profit-making company, how do profits depend on the library and its information? If the library is a traditional one in a non-profit-making organization, how do its presence and the services add to the prestige and value of the organization? These are the questions which can be explored with users, committees, and even with top management, and the awareness of the library and its value will thereby grow.

3. Will 'customers' buy what you are selling? Remember that information marketing is consumer-driven rather than product-driven. People want

solutions to their problems, not information for its own sake. No matter how many people give lip service to libraries as 'good', 'valuable', and 'important in our society', if those same people are not coming into your library, there is some reason. Does the library offer what they need, or what the organizational authorities and the librarian think they need?

4. Listen to your clientele. Opportunities and ideas for marketing often come from the target market itself. People do not necessarily know what they want from a particular service; try to get out of the library and talk to them. This will not only enable you to understand what they want, it will create good 'chemistry' between you and your users.

5. Always innovate. Differentiate what you have to offer from what others are offering. Otherwise, why should users come to you for their information needs?

6. Follow up. Find out how things you have innovated are working. Innovation without results is pointless.

7. Find out who benefits from the library, directly and indirectly, since part of your effort is going to involve using others to promote the library. You must have a clear understanding of who the library's users are, what proportion of the potential user population they constitute, and whether it is important or appropriate to make some effort to get the remaining user population into the library.

Marketing techniques

All libraries employ some form of promotion or public relations, either overtly or otherwise, but for the one-person librarian this is a highly effective way of affirming the importance of the library to the parent organization. It is at the same time a good means of evaluating the librarian's professional worth. Just as people are not going to use a library they never hear about, so they will not value the librarian if they do not know what goes on in the library. The discussion of the reference interview, which is, of course, the most direct communication between the librarian and the user, is one approach to marketing, but there are other targets for productive communication as well.

To reach management, one universally utilized form is the annual report. Whether it be a ten-page printed and bound booklet or a one-paragraph heading over some statistics, the annual report is probably the single most important document the one-person librarian will produce during the year. It is a statement which reflects the policies of the library, the accomplishments of the year and, significantly, goals for the future. It tells management what the librarian sees as problems and where the strengths of the library are to be found. Finally, it gives the library manager a tool to use in lobbying for changes, to build strengths and to eliminate weaknesses in the library operation. It is easy to underestimate the value of the annual report, to dismiss it as a chore, but management prefers to see the facts about the library and its services in black and white. For the alert and dynamic library manager who runs a library without help, compiling the annual report can be the most important task of the year.

It is important to prove to management and to users that a good library or information centre saves the valuable time of technical, professional and managerial staff. If the library receives inadequate funding, the annual report may go some way toward proving that more could be done if more money were allocated. The annual report can be used to put forward a positive case for the library, as well as for discussing what has already been accomplished. With the annual report, prepared for management but distributed to users and other interested parties as well, the library manager has an effective marketing tool.

Management briefings by the library manager are also important methods of communication. Management is concerned with all the operations of the organization, and while the library may not be high on the managerial list of necessary departments, it is up to the librarian to sell the library. He does this first by convincing management that the library's services are needed and appreciated. A good manager does not want to get involved in library operations – indeed, that is why she has hired a professional librarian – but she does want to know what is going on. Periodic briefings are invaluable to the manager, as they give a general picture of what the librarian is doing, and it is valuable for the librarian to let the manager know who uses the library, what interesting or useful questions are being asked, etc. By discussing problems, special circumstances, policy and other issues, the librarian gives management input about the library's value to the organization, which is certainly advantageous to the librarian.

Another valuable communication format is the written memorandum. In most organizations, the manager supervising the library keeps a file of current activities in the library, and as long as the librarian does not flood management with trivia, memos about projects and programmes will be appreciated. The memo also serves the purpose of keeping management informed when a personal briefing is not possible. Because of heavy demands on his time a manager might not be able to meet with the librarian as often as he would like, and a memo ensures that the information is conveyed. Similarly, in a difficult situation when the librarian and the manager are not getting along, the memo 'gets it down in writing', a less emotional communication technique that has been standard operating procedure in the business world for many years. The librarian should also share with management some of the complimentary letters he has received from satisfied users. Of course, the best public relations is the attitude of the librarian. In a one-person library a pleasant attitude is essential, because the librarian is the only one dealing with the user or manager, and it is the librarian who will effect a pleasant or an unpleasant reaction.

There are several communications tools which will be effective in bringing users into the library. Here again, the annual report can be the most useful of all, if it is well constructed and attractively presented. The users of the library are as entitled as management to know what the policies, services and goals of the library are. The report to users, if it is a separate one, could have a different emphasis, but many one-person librarians find that one annual report can serve both functions, with perhaps some special annotations for the version given to users.

We have said that good performance is effective public relations, and while this undoubtedly true, performance cannot be the *only* form of public relations. The manager of a one-person library needs constantly to remind users of the availability of the library services, and he or she must consider using promotional materials. These might be taken from a selection of the following: the annual report; a library guide; a periodic library newsletter; a weekly current-awareness bulletin; monthly accession lists; journal contents pages; abstracts from journals; bibliographies and reading lists; bulletin boards and articles for the organization's house journal or training newspaper. For a small public library, other promotional materials might be used, such as gift items with a library message, local newspaper or magazine publicity, or local television and radio advertising.

The ideal library guide comes in the form of a glossary, so busy users can scan it quickly to find areas of interest. For the library manager who decides to compile the guide in this form, there will need to be a short introduction giving a brief history of the library, it aims, hours of service and perhaps a short introduction to the staff. This should then be followed by the guide to the sources and how to use them, in alphabetical order. A short paragraph can be written about each topic.

The one-person librarian might also like to try compiling a weekly current-awareness bulletin. Some may consider this a time-consuming task, but it really only needs to be one side of a sheet giving short abstracts (a couple of lines will do) of items which may be of interest. Send this out regularly, and then photocopy the items at your leisure, so that other staff can come into the library to refer to them. Booklists and monthly accession lists are also invaluable, for these can be compiled without much effort even if you are desperately short of time. However, as with the current-awareness bulletin, the librarian must aim at providing booklists and monthly accession lists regularly, even if funding is minimal, as they are a valuable guide to what is new in the library, and users become accustomed to seeing them. They can be annotated if the librarian has time, and they are best done in a classified form. With a colourful cover and a short introduction, they can be effective marketing instruments for the one-person library.

Whether they are annotated or not, booklists or monthly acquisitions lists are valuable because they keep the picture of the library before clients and give them a feeling of knowing what is offered in the library, even if they are not immediately going to use it. The booklist can also serve as an important statistical tool, a point well made at one of the annual Elizabeth Ferguson Seminars in New York. Alice Norton, speaking on how to get people to use the library, remarked that the booklist can be a simple way of quantitatively evaluating how the library is used: we simply keep a record of the number of reservations that are made, and successfully filled, through the use of a regularly scheduled booklist.[10]

Other communications tools are received with varying degrees of success. Newsletters, with information about the library and its history and some of the special collections, are always popular, especially printed descriptions of work by users based on research undertaken at the library (provided of course that the presentation of such a description does not conflict with any particular regulations or rules about confidentiality, a consideration in a library which is part of the profit sector).

If the library is part of a larger organization, the librarian should make a point of contributing to the house organ on a regular basis. If he can write something interesting about the library once a month or quarterly, he should do so. Suitable subjects are staff accomplishments, visitors to the library, projects completed, meetings attended, and any work which will benefit users. The librarian can attach a short monthly report to the monthly accessions list, or send a short report to the line manager or senior management on a regular basis.

Marketing tips

Promotion includes more than the printed word. Michael LeBoeuf, writing about customer services, makes a strong case for what he calls 'first impressions', those brief opportunities we have to set the tone for what we are about.[11] His ideas can be adapted for the one-person library, and include the following:

- As soon as you see the user, politely acknowledge his/her presence.

- Be equally prompt and polite when answering the telephone.

- If a user has a scheduled appointment, make it your business to be on time.

- Prepare for a user's questions by having the answers, or at least a general idea about the user and his/her work, beforehand.

- Whenever possible, prepare in advance for each individual user (although, it must be recognized that this is not always possible in libraries which have a majority of 'walk-in' clients).

- Ask the right questions.

- Listen for total meaning – never underestimate the value of listening to a user.

- Match your solutions with the user's problems.

- Make the user feel good about using your library or information centre.

It is Charles Bauer, in his famous paper on 'Managing Management', who provides the one-person library with a no-nonsense approach to marketing:

> Using the same techniques practiced by any other business, you must advertise your services to create demand; sell aggressively to keep the turnover in the collection and the demand for services high; and keep users happy with good follow-up services. With these kinds of services, you establish yourself as an integral partner in the research and development team'.[12]

In the search for tips and techniques for marketing the one-person library, the library manager can turn to the American Marketing Association for a last set of guidelines. The Association distributes a pamphlet, '*Tips for the Effective Marketer*'[13] which can be usefully adapted for library purposes:

1. Be friendly and willing to help.

2. Treat each user as you would like to be treated.

3. Handle complaints quickly and professionally.

4. Be approachable.

5. Make it easy on the user.

6. Ask the user for his/her opinions.

7. Build a relationship with your users.

8. Never argue with a user.

9. If you don't know the answer to a user's question, immediately find someone who does.

10. Always try to do a little extra for the user.

11. Always be reliable – keep the service promise.

Finally though, the best way to market the one-person library is to raise its visibility, and steps for achieving this have been a recurrent theme throughout all that we have written about the one-person librarian and information services professional. It is all summed up in the essay referred to earlier, in which Gary Lance urged librarians to take the initiative in changing perceptions about their libraries.[14] Although the suggestions Lance made are geared specifically to news libraries, they can easily be adapted for use in any one-person library:

- Automate the library. Give management facts and figures; show them you know the technology. Get management involved with a library automation committee. No other single project has given the library greater visibility in the last few years.

- Survey your users. Nothing gives you more usable feedback than a poll of your users. Check out the Spring, 1988, issue of *Special Libraries* for an informative article on this topic.

- Attend newsroom or corporate meetings. Get out of the library! Learn how the other half lives. You may find that understanding how reporters and editors think can help you be a better librarian. But what's more important, corporate management will find that the library staff can make a contribution outside the library. Do anything you can to help break the isolation of the library.

- Hold library meetings, seminars, events. 'Meetings' is usually a dirty word in the newsroom, but how many of your reporters or editors have ever attended a seminar on library resources, a workshop session on personal filing systems, or an electronic library tutorial? Involve other departments also, with a library open house for all staff. Don't knock it 'til you've tried it.

- Represent your company in the community. A catchphrase in the newspaper business these days is 'serving the reader'. Get your library involved with reader service projects. A history project? A newspaper research guide? These are just some thoughts.

- Create a library newsletter. Publicize your achievements in words. New acquisitions, new databases, library automation updates, new services available are all good topics for the newsletter. If your company or newsroom has a newsletter, write a column for it or at least get mentioned in it occasionally.

- Publish informative guidelines. Subject bibliographies, lists of databases available to target groups such as the business department of the newspaper, a guide to the library, and an electronic library searching guide if you're automated are all good examples of library publications.

- Get published. If you're in print and this fact is brought to management's attention, it's bound to bring more attention to you and by association the library, especially in a word-oriented place like a newspaper. How about getting published in your newspaper? Several of your colleagues have done it.

- Give library awards. You can have fun with library awards. Give one to the reporter who is the most 'library literate'. How about an award to the reporter who most frequently reports on libraries or library services?

- Clean up the place. If your library is like most news libraries, it is probably not a place known for its aesthetic environment. Reorganize; restructure; move things around. How about some paint and carpeting? I know it takes money and a lot of 'elbow grease', but be creative. How about a reading area where staff can actually sit down with a newspaper or magazine away from their desks?

- Wow them with statistics. Some managers love numbers. If you've got a few of these types in your company, keep the numbers that will make your point. You'll be more visible to corporate management if you speak their language, i.e. the language of the 'bottom line' and 'cost justification'.

- Look at the profit potential of your library. Show management that you are producing revenue, e.g. newspaper microfilming, indexing sales, electronic library revenue, research service revenues. This is one to be careful with, however, or they may cut back your budget.

- Provide information leadership for your company. You know more about information than anyone in the company. Why don't they know what a valuable resource you are?

- Get crazy. Break out of the librarian stereotype, which is still all too real to most company management. Get mad when your library gets dumped on. Be vocal when it pays to be. Be visible to your company or news organization.

References

1 Pinchot, Gifford, *Intrapreneuring: Why You Don't Have to Leave the Corporation to Become an Entrepreneur*, Harper & Row, New York, 1985.

2 White, Herbert S., 'Entrepreneurship and the library profession,' *Journal of Library Administration* 8, (1), Spring 1987, p. 15.

3 Paul, Meg, 'Improving service provision,' *The Australian Library Journal*, February 1990, p. 65.

4 Wagner, Paul A., 'Marketing for NPOs – from a practitioner's point of view,' in: Patrick J. Montana (ed.) *Marketing in Non-profit Organizations*, ANACOM, New York, 1978, p. 40.

5 Wood, Lawraine, *Marketing Your Information Service*. Loughborough: Centre for Library and Information Management, 1985 (CLAIM Report No. 46).

6 Gothbert, Helen M., 'Understanding marketing – why you can't sell libraries like Kitty Litter,' *Library Administration and Management* 1, (2), March 1987, p. 56.

7 Kotler, Philip, *Marketing for Nonprofit Organizations*,   Prentice-Hall, Englewood Cliffs, NJ, 1975, p. x.

8 Edinger, Joyce A., 'Marketing library services: strategy for survival,' *College and Research Libraries*, 41, (4), July 1980. p. 329.

9 St. Clair, Guy, 'Marketing and promotion in today's special library,' *Aslib Proceedings*, 42, (7/8), July/August 1990, pp. 215–216.

10 Norton, Alice, Untitled remarks. A presentation delivered to the Elizabeth Ferguson Seminar. New York City Chapter, YWCA, and the New York Chapter, SLA, May 1984.

11 LeBoeuf, Michael, *How to Win Customers and Keep Them for Life*. G. P. Putnam's Sons, New York, 1988, p. 86.

12 Bauer, Charles, 'Managing management,' *Special Libraries*, April 1980.

13 *Marketing Is You*. American Marketing Association, Chicago, IL, 1988.

14 Lance, Gary, 'Improve your library's image,' *News Libraries News*, 11, (1), Fall 1988, pp. 3-4.

Chapter Fourteen

Afterword:
why work in a one-person library?

If there are so many people working in one-person libraries, why do we hear so little about them? Some have suggested – with tongue not so firmly in cheek – that one-person librarians are so busy they do not have time to write or even talk about their work. At one time this might not have been such a far-fetched idea, but nowadays we are not prepared to accept it wholeheartedly. For one thing, one of the purposes of this book has been to demonstrate that the one-person librarian can work alone and get the work done, if she follows certain rules about time management, communication, business practices and productive interactions with users and others who are affected by the library and its services.

Perhaps one reason we do not hear so much about one-person librarianship is that for many the job is an entry-level position, and employees often move on to a multistaff library before they have begun to deal seriously with or resolve the problems associated with one-person library management. Another reason might be that, in the past, the type of individual drawn to the one-person library was not assertive enough to obtain what he needed to achieve his goals. Certainly that has changed. A third reason probably has to do with the perception that non-librarians had of the profession. Prior to about 1965 or so, most managers, and indeed many users, had no concept of the professional skills needed to manage a library, even a library which employed only one person. That perception, too, has changed.

If there are so many problems in working in a one-person library, if there are so many professional and, possibly, personal inconsistencies, why would anyone do it? Why would anyone, trained for a service profession, want to work alone, where the opportunities of professional service are obviously limited, where there is absolutely no possibility for professional advancement within the organization and where, quite frankly, if he is not actively constantly fighting against it, he can get lost in a morass of clerical and other non-professional detail? There are two reasons, both having more to do with the personality of the library manager than with his training. First, there is definitely a lack of external pressure. For the librarian in a one-person library who does a good job, there is little of the harassing and political manoeuvering that characterizes many library positions. Any pressure is internal, based on a desire to do a good job and to keep up the good work, to meet the demands of the defined user groups served by the library. If the librarian wants to do so, he can make the library his own little world, and as long as he does a good job, is competent and keeps the users satisfied, he can be professionally happy without added pressure. Sometimes we call this lack of pressure 'independence', and, as we said earlier when we wrote about professional isolation, it is that independence that attracts so many people to jobs in one-person libraries. In that sense they are entrepreneurs, for they want to be in charge of their own operations, and they want to be rewarded for the successes that they themselves bring about. Independence is definitely a reason for working alone.

Another reason, of course, is appreciation. In the one-person library there is an immediate interaction between the user and the librarian, and even if the librarian is unable to finish the project and must refer the user elsewhere, the user is appreciative and will usually say so, either to the librarian or, better yet, to her manager (and frequently to both). The one-person library is a good place to work if the librarian wants to be appreciated and to see the results of her work.

Certainly not everyone would enjoy working in a one-person library. It is a special world, one that might be alien to an academic intellectual, to a skilled administrator or even to a librarian who wants to make a significant societal contribution. Yet for those who choose it, the tight-knit and pleasantly rewarding environment of the one-person library has advantages that far outweigh the problems.

While one-person librarians are to be found throughout the entire spectrum of librarianship and information services, the requirements for service in the one-person library align them closely with those libraries and information centres usually referred to as 'special' libraries. The techniques for success in the special library are the same as those employed in all successful one-person libraries, regardless of type. The one-person library, to all intents and purposes, is a special library, and the one-person librarian works as a special librarian.

There are those who would argue that it is the tenets and practices of special librarianship that will drive the library and information services profession in the 21st century. Patricia Berger, for example, a former president of the American Library Association, was asked to comment about the future of libraries and librarianship in the 90s and as we go into the 21st century. She remarked that 'the distinctions we have known in the past among the various kinds of libraries in this country will tend to disappear'.[1] Joseph Rosenthal, then University Librarian at the University of California, Berkeley, went even further and suggested that:

> Librarians will become more like special librarians. They will deal more in information and less in simply saying 'Here is the bibliographical apparatus; it's up to you to find out which things you want'. In certain situations, they may come to function more as part of a research team
> ...
>
> There will be different protocols for accessing data in these different

spheres or circles, and librarians will be kept busy trying to translate those protocols into simpler language for the researchers and trying to train people to use, to access, these different spheres of information.

The better librarians are at doing this, the more their services are going to be in demand. So to the extent that we and our successors are good, we will be building demand for our services.[1]

Even Frederick Kilgour, the man responsible for making OCLC the success it is in the library and information services profession, sees the future in special library terms. When asked, 'What will save libraries?' Kilgour responded: 'Supplying the information and knowledge that people want when and where they want it. Not just giving them a package and saying 'I hope you'll find what you want in here'

The interviewer then asked Kilgour, 'Are you saying that all libraries will have to become like the special library, where either you get the answer or you don't exist?' Kilgour responded: 'That's correct. I've been in librarianship for 50 years, and it's been the special librarians ...who have been the exciting people'.[1]

One-person librarians understand that we are living in an age of information and that our dependency on information will continue to grow. The faster we accept the fact that the library's role – whether it is a public, academic, school, or specialized library – is to lead its users to the information they need, the better the library and information services profession will be able to provide that information. And this, it seems to us, is the primary characteristic of the one-person librarian: she understands this distinction, understands that she is there to provide a service to her users, a service that will meet their needs.

So the one-person library is ready for the 21st century. We can safely assume that one-person libraries are going to be with us for a long time to come. There have always been small libraries, of course, and many more small libraries have grown up in the last few years to meet the information needs of various concerns and organizations. Are things getting better for the one-person librarian? Probably. We sense a camaraderie among one- person librarians that did not exist before, or if it existed no-one talked about it. People are now talking about what it is like to work alone, and they are attending workshops and seminars and continuing education courses on the subject. They are reading and writing articles about their experiences, and learning how to share resources and how to connect with one another so that the services of their libraries, small as they are, can be made available to as many users as they can find. They are interested, and with that interest they are bringing a commitment to a higher level of work for their employers, a higher sense of responsibility about the services they provide, and a strong sense of professionalism about their work (even among the many one-person librarians who do not have professional degrees).

As we have attempted to show in these pages, one-person librarians who succeed follow certain guidelines which contribute to their success. Perhaps the best summary of these was in response to a challenge to the editors of *The One-Person Library: A Newsletter for Librarians and Management*: What do you say, they were asked, to a one-person librarian who wants to know how to succeed? They had these suggestions:

1. Network. Network. Network. There is no other way to succeed in a one-person library. You must learn to ask for help from professional colleagues, friends, family members, co-workers, anyone who can be of service. And you must be willing to let them ask you.

2. Identify your advocates. There are people in your organization who like you, who approve of what you are doing, and who are keen to be associated with you. Learn who they are and seek their help when you need it. Those whom you support will support you.

3. Simplify. Simplify. Simplify. Cut through the layers. Just because some complicated arrangement works for another department or even another library or information centre, don't use it if it's too much trouble for the results you get.

4. Organize your time. No one-person librarian can afford the luxury of being casual about time management. Your time-management skills are as important as your searching (or budgeting or reference or processing) skills.

5. Think about how you are perceived. Remember you are the library to almost anyone who crosses your path. Do you present an image of the library that inspires confidence in your work, and more important, confidence in the information you organize and disseminate?

6. Soften up. If your sense of injustice is outraged because of some minor matter, stay cool. You are not the only employee on earth who doesn't always get what he or she wants (or needs). Save your energies for the big things. And in that case...

7. Get tough. The library is a vital part of the organization. And you are part of the team that makes things happen. Don't let yourself and your responsibility (your authority for managing the library) get pushed around. As far as the library is concerned, you're the boss and you set the standards. You know it and everyone else should too.

8. Maintain grace under pressure. And if you don't have it, acquire it. There's no one else to blow off steam with. You are in charge and whether it's a busted bookmobile axle or a computer service person who can't come for two days, you've got to live with it.

9. Take the rewards. And share them. Nobody, not even a one-person librarian, succeeds alone. When someone comes in to thank you for something that has helped them succeed, accept the compliment. And if someone has helped you to help them, include that person or that orga-

nization or those advocates in your kudos. Everyone likes to be recognized. And thanked.

10. Have some fun. Learn to enjoy what you do. One of the leaders in management says that those people who effect change in an organization are characterized by their playfulness. If you see something silly, giggle. Don't take it all so seriously.[2]

Considering the advances in modern technology and the reluctance of contemporary management personnel to add staff to library and information units in an organization, it is unlikely that the proportion of one-person librarians in the profession will fall to less than the current one-third to one-half per cent. In fact, it is probably safe to assume that the number of one-person operations will grow, as management comes to realize that one excellent, efficient and enthusiastic librarian or information services professional is preferable to two or more who do not provide the same level of service to users. It is these committed, enthusiastic librarians that their employers cannot help but appreciate, because they will bring to the parent organization, the community, the employing organization, hospital, society or teaching facility, good library service, which is all they wanted in the first place.

References

1 Riggs, Donald E. and Sabine, Gordon A., *Libraries in the 90s—What the Leaders Expect*, Oryx, Phoenix AZ, 1988, p. 2.

2 St. Clair, Guy, 'Thinking about... the keys to success,' *The One-Person Library: A Newsletter for Librarians and Management*, 7, (5), September 1990, p.4.

Bibliography

Ahrens, Barbara, 'Branch libraries,' in *Managing the Private Law Library, 1988*. New York: Practising Law Institute (1899), pp. 21-26.

Alley, Brian, and Jennifer Cargill. *Keeping Track of What You Spend: The Librarian's Guide to Simple Bookkeeping*. Phoenix, AZ: Oryx, 1982.

American Library Association, Library Administration Division, 'Guidelines for using volunteers in libraries,' *American Libraries*, 2, April, 407-408, 1971.

Aspnes, Grieg, 'A philosophy of special librarianship,' in Jackson, Eugene (ed.), *Special Librarianship: A New Reader*. Metuchen, New Jersey and London: The Scarecrow Press, 1980.

Association of American Library Schools, 'Policy statement on continuing library and information science education'. *Journal of Education for Librarianship*, 21 (4) 1981.

Anthony, L.J., ed. *Handbook of Special Librarianship and Information Work*. London: Aslib, 1982.

Ashworth, Wilfred. *Special Librarianship*. Outlines of Modern Librarianship. London: Clive Bingley, 1979.

Barclay, Ian. 'Time management.' Paper delivered at the Library Association Industrial Group Annual Conference, York, March 1984.

Barnes, Robert F. 'Some thoughts on professional ethics codes,' in *ASIS Bulletin*, April/May, 1986, pp. 19-20.

Bauer, Charles K. 'Managing management,' in *Special Libraries*, 71 (4) April, 1980, pp. 204-216.

Beaufien, Anne K., comp. *Fee-Based Services: Issues & Answers: Second Conference on Fee-Based Research in College and University Libraries*. Ann Arbor, MI: Michigan Information Transfer Source, 1987.

Bell, Steven J. 'Cutback management for special libraries: strategies for library survival,' in *Special Libraries*, July, 1984, pp. 205-213.

Bender, David R., Kadec, Sarah T. and Morton, Sandy I. *National Information Policies: Strategies for the Future*. Washington, DC: Special Libraries Association, 1991.

Bennis, Warren. *On Becoming a Leader*. Boston: Addison-Wesley, 1989.

Bennis, Warren. *Why Leaders Can't Lead*. San Francisco: Jossey-Bass, 1990.

Bennis, Warren, and Nanus, Burt. *Leaders: The Strategies for Taking Charge*. New York: Harper and Row, 1985.

Benson, Joseph, 'Networking: the new wave for special librarians,' *Special Librarianship: A New Reader*. Metuchen, New Jersey: The Scarecrow Press, 1980, p. 380.

Berger, Patricia W. 'Federal Government libraries and information centers,' in *Education for Professional Librarians*, edited by Herbert S. White. White Plains, NY: Knowledge Industry Publications, 1986, pp. 141-154.

Berner, Andrew. 'Collection development,' remarks delivered at The University Club of New York, Library Associates, March, 1983.

Berner, Andrew. 'The importance of time management in the small library.' *Special Libraries*, 78 (4), Fall, 1987.

Berner, Andrew 'Thinking about ... surviving the 90s' *The One–Person Library: A Newsletter for Librarians and Management* 6, (7), Nov. 1989, p.4

Berner, Andrew. *Time Management in the Small Library: A Computer-Assisted Study Program*. Washington, DC: Special Libraries Association, 1988.

Berner, Andrew and St. Clair, Guy (eds), *The Best of OPL: Five Years of* The One–Person Library. Washington, D.C.: Special Libraries Association, 1990.

Bishop, Ashton C. and Rasoul H. Tondkar. 'Development of a professional code of ethics.' *Journal of Accountancy*, May, 1987, pp. 97-100.

Blagden, J. 'Financial management,' in Anthony, L.J. (ed.), *Handbook of Special Librarianship and Information Work*. London: Aslib, 1982.

Blewett, Laurel A. 'Part of the team: profile of a pediatric librarian,' *The One-Person Library* 7 (1) May, 1990, pp. 2-4.

Blixrud, Julia C. and Edmund J. Sawyer. 'A Code of Ethics for ASIS,' *Bulletin of the American Society for Information Science*, October, 1984, pp. 8-10.

Bolef, Doris. 'The Special Library,' in *The How-to-do-it Manual for Small Libraries*. New York: Neal-Schuman, 1988.

The Bottom Line: A Financial Magazine for Librarians. New York: Neal-Schuman, 1986–

Brimsek, Tobi, comp. *From the Top: Profiles of U.S. and Canadian Corporate Libraries and Information Centers*. Washington, DC: Special Libraries Association, 1989.

Brimsek, Tobi, comp. *Inside Information: Profiles of Association Libraries and Information Centers*. Washington, DC: Special Libraries Association, 1991.

Brimsek, Tobi., comp. *Powering Up: A Technological Assessment of the SLA Membership*. Washington, DC: Special Libraries Association, 1990.

Brown, Carol R. *Selecting Library Furniture: A Guide for Librarians, Designers, and Architects*. Phoenix, AZ: Oryx, 1989.

Bruemmer, Alice, Reed, Janet and Quinn, Karen Takle, eds. *Library Management in Review*. New York: Special Libraries Association, 1981.

Bullard, Scott R. 'Ethics of vendor-library relations,' in *Library Acquisitions Practice and Theory* 8, 1984, pp. 251-254.

Burkett, J., 'Library and information networks', *Handbook of Special Librarianship and Information Work*. London: Aslib, 1982.

Burwasser, Suzanne M. *File Management Handbook for Managers and Librarians*. Studio City, CA: Pacific Information, Inc., 1986.

Calano, Jimmy and Salzman, Jeff. 'How to get more done in a day,' *Working Woman*, April, 1988.

Campbell, William D. *A Budgeting Manual for Small Public Libraries*. Clarion, PA: The Center for the Study of Rural Librarianship and the Small Library Development Center, 1987.

Caputo, Janette S. *Stress and Burnout in Library Service*. Phoenix, AZ: Oryx, 1991.

Christianson, Elin B. 'Corporate Libraries'. In *Education for Professional Librarians*, edited by Herbert S. White. White Plains, NY: Knowledge Industry Publications, 1986, pp. 89-104.

Christianson, Elin B., King, David E. and Ahrensfeld, Janet L., *Special Libraries: A Guide for Management*. Washington, DC: Special Libraries Association, 1991.

Cirano, Paul John. *The Business of Running a Library*. Jefferson, NC: McFarland, 1991.

Close to the Customer: An American Management Association Research Report on Consumer Affairs. New York: American Management Association, 1987.

Cohen, Jeffrey R. and Turner, Robert M. 'Ethics and Professionalism: The CPA in industry,' in *CPA*, April, 1990, pp. 42-49.

Cohen, William A. *The Art of the Leader*. Englewood Cliffs, NJ: Prentice-Hall, 1990.

'Coming of Age,' *Inc.*, 11, (4), 39, April, 1989.

'Concerning time management: some thoughts on interruptions.' *The One-Person Library: A Newsletter for Librarians and Management* 3 (1), May, 1986, pp.1-2.

Coopers and Lybrand. *A challenge to complacency: changing attitudes to training*. Coopers and Lybrand, 1986.

Corbin, John. *Implementing the Automated Library System*. Phoenix, AZ: Oryx, 1988.

Crawford, Helen. 'In search of an ethic of medical librarianship,' in *Bulletin of the Medical Library Association* 66 (3) July, 1978, pp. 331-337.

Creth, Sheila and Frederick Duda. *Personal Administration in Libraries*. New York: Neal-Schuman, 1989.

Crosby, Philip B. *Let's Talk Quality*. New York: Penguin Books, 1990.

Crosby, Philip B. *Quality is Free*. New York: Penguin Books, 1979.

Crosby, Philip B. *Quality With Tears: The Art of Hassle-Free Management*. New York: McGraw-Hill, 1984.

Curzon, Susan C. *Managing Change: A How-to-do-it Manual for Planning, Implementing and Evaluating Change in Libraries*. New York: Neal-Schuman, 1989.

Dalziel, Murray M. and Schoonover, Stephen C. *Changing Ways: A Practical Tool for Implementing Change Within Organizations.* New York: American Management Association, 1988.

Deal, Terence, and Kennedy, Allan. *Corporate Cultures: The Rites and Rituals of Corporate Life.* Boston, MA: Addison–Wesley, 1982.

Dean, Sharon. *Winning Marketing Techniques: An Introduction to Marketing for Information Professionals.* Washington, DC. Special Libraries Association, 1990.

Doherty, Walter E. , 'How to turn a library into a profit center: The law library example,' in *The Bottom Line Reader: A Financial Handbook for Librarians.* New York: Neal-Schuman, 1990, pp. 141-142.

Downes, Robin N. 'Managing for innovation in the age of information technology,' *Journal of Library Administration* 8 (1) 1987, pp. 77-84.

Drabenstott, Jon. 'Ethics in the library automation process,' *Library Hi-Tech*, 16, pp. 107-119.

Drake, David, 'When your boss isn't a librarian,' *American Libraries*, February, 1990. pp. 152–153.

Drucker, Peter. *The Effective Executive.* New York: Harper and Row, 1966.

Dunckel, Jacqueline, and Taylor, Brian. *Keeping Customers Happy: Strategies for Success.* North Vancouver, BC: International Self-Counsel Press, Ltd., 1988.

Duston, Beth, and St. Clair, Guy. 'Opportunities: mining the company library,' *Growth Strategies: Managing Change for Profits* 2 (1) American Management Association, November, 1987.

East, Harry, 'Changes in the staffing of UK special libraries and information services in the decade 1972-1981: a review of the DES census data,' *Journal of Documentation*, 39, (4), 247-265, 1983.

Eaton, Nancy L., MacDonald, Linda Brew and Saule, Mara R. *CD-ROM and Other Optical Information Systems: Implementation Issues for Libraries.* Phoenix, AZ: Oryx, 1989.

Echelman, Shirley. 'Libraries are businesses, too!' *Special Libraries*, 65 (Oct./Nov. 1974), pp. 410-417. Also re-printed in Jackson, *op.cit.*, pp. 151-158.

Edinger, Joyce A. 'Marketing library services: strategy for survival,' *College and Research Libraries* 41 (4) July, 1980, pp. 328-332.

Epstein, Susan Baerg. 'Ethical considerations in an sutomated environment,' in *Library Journal*, September 15, 1990, pp. 59-60.

Esrey, William. 'Improving productivity,' Keynote Address at the White House Conference on Library and Information Services, Washington, D.C., July 19, 1991.

Evans, G. Edward. *Management Techniques for Librarians.* New York: Academic Press, 1976.

Expert Systems and Library Applications (An SLA Information Kit). Washington, DC: Special Libraries Association, 1991.

Ferguson, Elizabeth and Mobley, Emily R., *Special Libraries at Work*, Hamden, Connecticut: Library Professional Publications, an imprint of The Shoe String Press, Inc., 1984.

Finks, Lee W. 'Librarianship needs a new code of professional ethics,' *American Libraries*, January, 1991, pp. 34-92.

Fox, Beth Wheeler. *Behind the Scenes at the Dynamic Library*. Chicago: American Library Association, 1990.

Fox, Beth Wheeler. *The Dynamic Community Library: Creative, Practical, and Inexpensive Ideas for the Director*. Chicago: ALA, 1988.

Frederick, William C. 'An ethics roundtable,' *Management Review*, August, 1988, pp. 48-50.

Freifeld, Roberta, and Masyr, Caryl. *Space Planning in the Special Library*. Washington, DC: Special Libraries Association, 1991.

Friese, Diane, and Westerlund, Christina, eds. *Libraries in Utility Commissions: Creation, Evaluation and Use*. Augusta, ME: Public Utilities Commission Information Resource Network, 1990.

Froehlich, Thomas J. [Letter to the Editor] *Bulletin of the American Society for Information Science*, October/November, 1990, p.4.

Future Competences of the Information Professional. Washington, DC: Special Libraries Association, 1991.

Gabarro, John J. & Kotter, John P. *Managing Your Boss. HBR Classic NO 80104*, Cambridge, MA: Harvard Business Review, 1979.

Garrett, Marie. 'Applied and professional ethics: resources for research,' in *Reference Quarterly*, Summer, 1990, pp. 497-503.

Gates, Jean Key. 'Special libraries' in *Introduction to Librarianship*, New York: Neal-Schuman Publishers, 1990. pp. 195-200.

Gellermann, William, Frankel, Mark S. and Ladenson, Robert F. *Values and Ethics in Organizations and Human Systems Development: Responding to Dilemmas in Professional Life*. San Francisco: Jossey-Bass, 1990.

Gensel, Susan and Powers, Audrey, 'Collection development and the special library.' *The New York State Library Bookmark*, 41 (1), Fall, 1982, p. 11.

Georgi, Charlotte, and Bellanti, Robert. Excellence in Library Management, *Journal of Library Administration*, 6 (3) 1985.

Gertzog, Alice, ed. *Leadership in the Library/Information Profession*. Jefferson, NC: McFarland, 1989.

Gervasi, Anne, and Seibt, Betty Kay, *Handbook for Small, Rural and Emerging Public Libraries*. Phoenix, AZ: Oryx, 1988.

Gervino, Joan. 'Put information to work for you,' *Association Management*, February, 1989, pp. 175-178.

Golden, Fay Ann. 'The ethics of reference service,' *Journal of Library Administration*, 1990, pp. 157-166.

Goldzimer, Linda Silverman. *'I'm First: Your Customer's Message to You.'* New York: Berkeley Books, 1989.

Gorman, Michael. 'Laying siege to the fortress library: a vibrant technological web connecting resources and users will spell its end.' *American Libraries* 17, (5), 325-328, 1986.

Gothbert, Helen M. 'Understanding marketing—why you can't sell libraries like Kitty Litter,' *Library Administration and Management* 1 (2), March, 1987.

Gross, Malvern J. and Warshauer, William, Jr. *Financial and Accounting Guide for Nonprofit Organizations*. New York: John Wiley and Sons, 1979.

Guaspari, John. *The Customer Connection: Quality for the Rest of Us*. New York: American Management Association. 1988.

Guide to Career Opportunities for Special Librarians and Information Professionals, 1991 (An SLA Information Kit). Washington, DC: Special Libraries Association, 1991.

Hauptman, Robert. *Ethical Challenges in Librarianship*. Phoenix: Oryx, 1988.

Herman, Larry. 'Costing, charging and pricing: related but different decisions,' *The Bottom Line*, 4 (2), pp. 26-28.

Hull, Nina N., 'Hospital OPLs face the 90s,' *The One-Person Library: A Newsletter for Librarians and Management* 7 (6) October, 1990, pp. 3-5.

Hurych, Jitka M. and Glenn, Ann C., 'Ethics in health sciences librarianship,' *Bulletin of the Medical Library Association* 75 (4) October, 1987, pp. 342-348.

Information: A Strategy for Economic Growth: Papers Presented at the State-of-the-art Institute, November 6-8, 1989, Washington, DC. Washington, DC: Special Libraries Association, 1990.

[Information Centers] The 1986 American Management Association Report on Information Centers. New York: American Management Association, 1986.

The Information Professional: An Unparalleled Resource: Papers Contributed for the 81st Annual Conference of the Special Libraries Association, June 9-14, 1990, Pittsburgh, PA. Washington, DC: Special Libraries Associaton, 1990.

Information 2000—Library and Information Services for the 21st Century: Summary Report of the 1991 White House Conference on Library and Information Services. Washington, DC, 1991.

Insights on Information Brokering (An SLA Information Kit). Washington, DC: Special Libraries Association, 1991.

Jackson, Eugene B., ed. *Special Librarianship: A New Reader*. Metuchen, NJ & London: The Scarecrow Press, 1980.

Jenkins, Harold. 'The library volunteer: volunteers in the future of libraries,' *Library Journal*, 97, 15 April, 1399-1403, 1972.

Johnson, Doris E. 'The information center: necessity or luxury?' *The One-Person Library: A Newsletter for Librarians and Management* 4 (1) May, 1987. pp. 1-3.

Kanter, Rosabeth Moss. *The Change Masters*. New York: Touchstone (S&S), 1985.

Katayama, Jane H. 'The library committee: how important is it?' *Special Libraries* 24 (1) January, 1983, pp. 44-49.

King, Geraldine. *Reference Service in the Small Library*. Chicago: ALA, 1985.

Koch, Heidi C., 'Criteria–based performance evaluations for hospital managers,' *Special Libraries* 80, (4) Fall, 1989, p. 272.

Kochen, Manfred. 'Opinion paper: ethics and information science,' *Journal of the American Society for Information Science*, 38 (3), 1987, pp. 206-210.

Koenig, Michael. *Budgeting Techniques for Libraries and Information Centers*. Professional Development Series, v. 1. New York: Special Libraries Association, c. 1980.

Koenig, Michael, ed. *Managing the Electronic Library: Papers of the 1982 Conference of the Library Management Division of the Special Libraries Association*. New York: Special Libraries Association, 1983.

Kok, John, 'Now that I'm in charge, what do I do?' *Special Libraries*, 71 (12): 523–528, Dec. 1980.

Kotler, Philip. *Marketing for nonprofit organizations*. Englewood Cliffs, NJ: Prentice-Hall, 1975.

Labovitz, Judith. 'Managing a special library,' *Journal of Library Administration*, 1985.

Ladendorf, Janice. 'Information service evaluation: the gap between the ideal and the possible,' *Special Libraries* 64 (7) July, 1973, pp. 273-279.

Lakein, Alan. *How to Get Control of Your Time and Your Life*. New York: New American Library, 1973.

Lance, Gary. 'Improve your library's image,' *News Libraries News* 11 (1) Fall, 1988.

LaRosa, Sharon M. 'Fees for service: the silver lining,' *MLS: Marketing Library Services* 5 (1) February/March, 1991, pp. 1-4.

LeBoeuf, Michael. *How to Win Customers and Keep Them for Life*. New York: Berkeley Books, 1985.

LeBoeuf, Michael. *Working Smart: How to Accomplish More in Half the Time*. New York: Warner, 1979.

Leerburger, Benedict A. *Marketing the Library*. White Plains, NY: Knowledge Industry Publications, 1982.

Libraries in the Age of Automation: A Reader for the Professional Librarian. White Plains, NY: Knowledge Industry Publications, 1986.

Loo, Shirley, ed. *Management by Design*. New York: Special Libraries Association, 1982.

Love, Erika. 'Medical libraries,' *Education for Professional Librarians*, edited by Herbert S. White. White Plains, NY: Knowledge Industry Publications, 1986, pp. 105-122.

MacDonald, Arley Ripin. *Managers View Information*. New York: Special Libraries Association, 1983.

Machalow, Robert. *Using Lotus 1-2-3: A How-to-do-it Manual for Library Applications*. New York: Neal-Schuman, 1989.

Mackenzie, Alec and Waldo, Kay Cronkite. *About Time! A Woman's Guide to Time Management*. New York: McGraw-Hill, 1981.

Mackenzie, R. Alex. *The Time Trap: How to Get More Done in Less Time*. New York: McGraw-Hill, 1972.

Mackie, Karl J. 'Business regulation, business ethics and the professional employee,' *Journal of Business Ethics*, 8, 1989, pp. 607-616.

Madaus, J. Richard. 'Academic library funding and professional ethics,' *College and Research Libraries News*, November, 1987, pp. 606-609.

Madsen, Peter, and Jam M. Shafritz. *Essentials of Business Ethics*. New York: Meridien, 1990.

Manning, Helen M., 'The corporate librarian: great return on investment,' in *Information: A Strategy for Economic Growth*, Papers Presented at the State-of-the-Art Institute, November 6-8, 1989, Washington, DC (Washington, DC: Special Libraries Association, 1990)..

Marketing is you. Chicago, IL: American Marketing Association, 1988.

Martin, Murray S. (ed.), *Financial Planning for Librarians*. New York: The Haworth Press, 1983.

Mason, J. Barry, William O. Bearden, and Lynne Davis Richardson. 'Perceived conduct and professional ethics among marketing faculty,' *Journal of the Academy of Marketing Science*, 18 (3) Summer, 1990, pp. 185-197.

Masterminding Tomorrow's Information—Creative Strategices for the '90s: Professional Papers from the 82nd Annual Conference of the Special Libraries Association, June 8-13, 1991, San Antonio, TX. Washington, DC: Special Libraries Association, 1991.

Matarazzo, James M., *Corporate Library Excellence*. Washington, DC: Special Libraries Association, 1990.

Matarazzo, James M., Prusak, Laurence, and Gauthier, Michael R. *Valuing Corporate Libraries: A Survey of Senior Managers*. Washington, DC: Special Libraries Association, 1990.

Mintz, Anne P. 'Ethics and the news librarian,' in *Special Libraries*, 82 (1) Winter, 1991, pp. 7–11.

Mintz, Anne P., ed. *Information Ethics: Concerns for Librarianship and the Information Industry*. Jefferson, NC: McFarland, 1990.

Mintz, Anne P. 'Quality control and the zen of database production,' *Online*, November, 1990, pp. 15-23.

'MLA code of ethics drafted,' in *MLA News*, 239, October, 1991, pp. 1,4.

Morton, Phillip W. 'The information manager: a link in effective organizational decision making,' in Koenig, *Managing the Electronic Library. op.cit.*

Moskowitz, Robert. *How to Organize Your Life and Your Work*. Garden City, NY: Doubleday, 1981.

Mount, Ellis. *Special Libraries and Information Centres: An Introductory Text*. Washington, DC: Special Libraries Association, 1991.

Nader, Julie. 'How special are 'special' libraries?' *The One-Person Library: A Newsletter for Librarians and Management* 7 (10) February, 1991, pp. 2-5..

National Commission on Libraries and Information Science/Special Libraries Association Task Force. *The Role of the Special Library in Networks and Cooperatives: Executive Summary and Recommendation*. New York: Special Libraries Association, 1984.

National Economic Development Council/Manpower Services Commission. *Training and Education in the Federal Republic of Germany, the United States and Japan*. NEDC/MSC, 1984.

'Negotiating: getting (close to) what you want,' in *The One-Person Library: A Newsletter for Librarians and Management* 7 (10) February, 1991, pp. 1-2.

Networking and Special Libraries (An SLA Information Kit). Washington, DC: Special Libraries Association, 1990.

'The new communications: variety and impact—part one,' *The One-Person Library: A Newsletter for Librarians and Management* 2 (4) August, 1985.

'A new survey: salaries and other data,' *The One–Person Library: A Newsletter for Librarians and Management*, 5, 4, 2, August, 1988.

Newman, William H. and Harvey W. Wallender. 'Managing not-for-profit enterprises,' *Academy of Management Review*, 3 (1), 24-31, 1978.

Nitecki, Joseph Z. 'The predicament of hypocrisy in librarianship,' in *Catholic Library World*, May/June, 1983, pp. 406-411.

Norton, Alice. Untitled remarks. A presentation delivered to the Elizabeth Ferguson Seminar. New York City Chapter, YWCA, and the New York Chapter, SLA, May, 1984.

O'Donnell, William S. 'The vulnerable corporate special library/information center: minimizing the risks,' *Special Libraries* 67 (April, 1976), p. 179-180.

The One–Person Library: A Newsletter for Librarians and Management. New York: OPL Resources, Ltd. [Murray Hill Station P.O. Box 948 New York, NY 10156], 1984–

Open University Committee on Continuing Education. *Report of the Committee on Continuing Education*. Open University, Milton Keynes, UK. 1975.

Orna, Elizabeth. 'Should we educate our users?' *Aslib Proceedings*, 30, (4), 132, 1978.

Palmer, Richard Phillips and Varnet, Harvey. *How to Manage Information: A Systems Approach*. Phoenix, AZ: Oryx, 1990.

Parson, Mary Jean. *Back to Basics: Planning*. New York: Facts on File, 1985.

Paul, Meg. 'Improving service provision,' *The Australian Library Journal*, February, 1990.

Penniman, W. David. *Preparing for Future Information Delivery Systems*, the Second Annual John T. Corrigan Memorial Lecture, 3 May 1991. Washington, DC: The Council of National Library and Information Associations, CNLIA Occasional Paper No. 2.

Perkins, David L. (ed.), *Guidelines for Collection Development*, American Library Association, Collection Development Committee, Resources and Technical Services Division, Chicago, 1979.

Peterson, Kenneth G. 'Ethics in academic librarianship: the need for values,' *The Journal of Academic Librarianship* 9 (3) 1983, pp. 132-137.

Pfeifer, Cheryl. 'Redefining the role of the information specialist in response to technology,' In The *information professional: an unparalleled resource, Papers Contributed for the 81st Annual Conference of the Special Libraries Association, June 9-14, 1990, Pittsburgh, PA.* Washington, DC: Special Libraries Association, 1991.

Pinchot, Gifford III. *Intrapreneuring: Why you don't have to leave the corporation to become an entrepreneur,* New York: Harper & Row, 1985.

Preer, Jean. 'Special ethics for special librarians?' *Special Libraries,* 82 (1) Winter, 1991, pp. 12-18.

Prentice, Ann E. 'Professional ethics,' *Catholic World,* November, 1984, pp. 130-133.

'President Nemeyer: Seeking good connections [1982 ALA Annual Conference Inaugural Address]' *American Libraries,* 13, (9), 531, 1982.

President's Task Force on the Value of the Information Professional. Final Report. Preliminary Study. Washington, D.C.: Special Libraries Association, 1987.

Private Law Libraries: Survey of Compensation. American Association of Law Libraries Private Law Libraries/Special Interest Section. Washington, DC: Special Libraries Association, 1991.

'Professional Ethics [Special Issue],' *Journal of Counseling and Development* 64 (5) January, 1986.

Prytherch, Ray (ed.). *Handbook of library training practice.* Volume 2. London: Gower Press, 1990.

Rainey, Nancy B. 'Ethical principles and liability risks in providing drug information,' *Medical Reference Services Quarterly* 7 (3) 1988, pp. 59-67.

Reck, Ross R. *Turn Your Customers Into Your Sales Force: The Art of Winning Repeat and Referral Customers.* New York: Prentice-Hall, 1991.

Riggs, Donald E. and Sabine, Gordon A. eds. *Libraries in the '90s: What the Leaders Expect.* Phoenix, AZ: Oryx, 1988.

Riggs, Donald E., ed. *Creativity, Innovation, and Entrepreneurship in Libraries,* in *Journal of Library Administration,* 10 (2/3) 1989.

Ross, Catherine Sheldrick, and Dewdney, Patricia. *Communicating Professionally: A How-to-do-it Manual for Librarians.* New York: Neal-Schuman, 1989.

Rouse. William B. and Rouse, Sondra H., *Management of Library Networks: Policy Analysis, Implementation and Control.* New York: Wiley, 1981

St. Clair, Guy. 'Commitment, courage and a lot of heart: management strategies for the dmall library,' in *Bibliotheca Medica Canadiana,* 8 (3) 1988, pp. 139-143.

St. Clair, Guy. 'Interpersonal networking: It is who you know,' *Special Libraries,* 80, (2), 108, Spring, 1989.

St. Clair, Guy. 'Library management: what does it mean to you?' *Library Management Quarterly,* 9 (4) Spring, 1986.

St. Clair, Guy. 'Marketing and promotion in today's special library,' *Aslib Proceedings* 42 (7/8), July/August, 1990, pp. 213-217. Also re-printed in *The One-Person Library* 7 (6) October, 1990, pp. 1-3, and 7 (7) November, 1990, pp. 5-7.

St. Clair, Guy. 'The new literacy: do special librarians have a role?' *Special Libraries* 82 (2) Spring, 1991, pp. 99-105.

St. Clair, Guy. 'The one-person library: an essay on essentials,' *Special Libraries* 67 (5-6) (May/June, 1976), pp. 233-238. Also re-printed in Jackson, *op.cit.*, pp. 171-177.

St. Clair, Guy. 'The one-person library: an essay on essentials revisited,' *Special Libraries* 78 (4) (Fall, 1987), pp. 263-270. Also re-printed in Hannigan, Jane Anne, ed. *Library Lit. 19— The Best of 1988*. Metuchen, NJ and London: The Scarecrow Press, 1989, pp. 362-371.

St. Clair, Guy. 'Thinking about... the keys to success,' *The One-Person Library: A Newsletter for Librarians and Management*, 7 (5), September, 1990, p.4.

St. Clair, Guy. 'Thinking about... WHCLIS and the one-person library,' *The One-Person Library: A Newsletter for Librarians and Management*, 8 (4), August, 1991, p.7.

St. Clair, Guy and Williamson, Joan, *Managing the One-Person Library*. London and New York: Bowker-Saur, 1986.

A Sampler of Forms for Special Libraries. Washington, DC: Special Libraries Association, 1991.

Saunders, W.L. *Towards a unified professional organization for library and information science services: a personal view*. Viewpoints on LIS 3. London: The Library Association, 1989.

Savan, Beth. 'Beyond professional ethics: issues and agendas,' *Journal of Business Ethics* 8, 1989, pp. 179-185.

Schuyler, Michael and Hoffman, Jake. *PC Management: A How-to-do-it Manual for Selecting, Organizing, and Managing Personal Computers in Libraries*. New York: Neal-Schuman, 1990 .

Segal, JoAn S. 'Special libraries and multitype networks,' *Special Libraries* 80, (2), 91, Spring, 1989.

Sellen, Betty-Carol, and Turock, Betty J., (eds.), *The Bottom Line Reader: A Financial Handbook for Librarians*. New York: Neal-Schuman, 1990.

Serjean, R., 'Librarianship and information work: job characteristics and staffing needs,' *British Library R&D Report 5321 HC*, London, 1973.

Shaughnessy, Thomas W. 'Making the boss more effective,' *Journal of Library Administration*, 8 (2) 1987, pp. 5-14.

Shaughnessy, Thomas W. 'Organizational culture in libraries: some managment perspectives,' *Journal of Library Administration* 9 (3) 1988, pp. 5-9.

Shaughnessy, Thomas W. 'The search for quality,' *Journal of Library Administration*, 8 (1) 1987, pp. 5-9.

Shea, Gordon F. *Company Loyalty: Earning It, Keeping It*. New York: American Management Association, 1987.

Shea, Gordon F. *Practical Ethics*. New York: American Management Association, 1988.

Shein, Edgar. *Organizational Culture and Leadership: A Dynamic View*. San Francisco: Jossey–Bass, Inc. and London: Jossey–Bass, Ltd., 1985.

Shuter, J. and Collins, J., 'The isolated professional,' *Information and Library Manager*, 3, (4), 106, 1984.

Sichel, Beatrice, 'Utilizing student assistants in small libraries,' *Journal of Library Administration*, 3, (1), p. 36, 1982.

Sinclair, Dorothy. *The Administration of the Small Public Library*. Chicago, Illinois: American Library Association, 1979.

Slater, Margaret. *'Investment in training: a quick, qualitative conspection in the library-information field.'* British Library R&D Report 6048, BLRDD, 1991.

Special Libraries. Washington, DC: Special Libraries Association, 1909-

[Special Libraries Association] President's Task Force on the Value of the Information Professional. Final Report. Washington, DC: Special Libraries Association, 1987.

[Special Libraries Association] SLA Biennial Salary Survey—1991. Washington, DC: Special Libraries Association, 1991.

[Special Libraries Association] SLA Triennial Salary Survey—1986 . Washington,D.C.: Special Libraries Association, 1986.

Smith, Stevenson G. *Accounting for Librarians and Other Not-for-Profit Managers*. Chicago: American Library Association, 1983.

Stevens, Norman. 'The new ethics,' *Library Hi-Tech*, 16, pp. 49-51.

Stichler, Richard N. 'On reforming ALA's code of ethics,' in *American Libraries*, January, 1992, pp. 40-44.

Strable, Edward G. 'The way it was,' in *The Special Library Role in Networks*. ed, Robert W. Gibson, New York: Special Libraries Association, 1980.

Swanigan, Meryl, 'Managing a special library, Part II,' *Excellence in Library Management (Journal of Library Management)*, 6 (3) p. 17, Fall, 1985,

Talcott, Ann W. 'A case study in adding intellectual value: the executive information service,' *The President's Task Force on the Value of the Information Professional Final Report Preliminary Study*. Washington, D.C.: Special Libraries Association, 1987.

Thomas, Lou. 'A Special Librarian's View of Funding: Selling Your Library to Management,' in *Louisiana Library Bulletin*, Spring, 1984, pp. 133-135.

Tools of the Profession. Washington, DC: Special Libraries Association, 1991.

Varlejs, Jana, ed. *The Economics of Information*. Jefferson, NC: McFarland, 1982.

Vogelsang, Marlene. 'The reflection of corporate culture in the library or information center,' *Library Management Quarterly*, Spring, 1989, pp. 16–20.

Wagner, Paul A. 'Marketing for NPOs—from a practitioner's point of view,' in *Marketing in non-profit organizations*, Patrick J. Montana (ed.) New York: ANACOM, 1978.

Waldron, Helen J. 'The business of running a special library,' *Special Libraries*, 62 (Feb. 1971): 66.

Warner, Alice Sizer, *Volunteers in Libraries II*, Library Journal Special Report #24, New York: Bowker, 1983.

Webb, Sylvia P. *Best practice? Continuing professional development for library/information staff in UK professional firms.'* British Library R&D Report 6039. Berkhamsted, Herts: Sylvia Webb, 1991.

Webb, Sylvia P., *Creating an Information Service*. London: Aslib, 1983.

Weingard, D.C. . 'The information hotseat: continuing education in a changing world,' *Journal of Education for Librarianship*, 24 (4) 1984.

Wessell, Deborah. *Grace Under Pressure: Writing with Clarity, Conciseness and Impact*. Washington, DC: Special Libraries Association, 1989.

'When a salesman comes to call' *The One-Person Library: A Newsletter for Librarians and Management* 1 (8) December, 1984, pp. 2-3.

White, Herbert S. 'Entrepreneurship and the library profession,' *Journal of Library Adminstration*, 8 (1) 1987, pp. 11-28.

White, Herbert S. *Librarians and the Awakening from Innocence: A Collection of Papers*. Boston: G.K. Hall, 1989.

White, Herbert S. *Managing the Special Library: Strategies for Success within the Larger Organization*. White Plains, NY: Knowledge Industry Publications, 1984.

White, Herbert S. 'Basic competencies and the pursuit of equal opportunity, part 7', *Library Journal*, 113, (12), pp. 56-57.

Wilson, Pauline, *Stereotype and Status: Librarians in the United States*, Contributions in Librarianship and Information Science, Number 41. Westport, Connecticut: Greenwood Press, 1932.

Willard, Ann M. and Morrison, Patricia. 'The dynamic role of the information specialist: two perspectives,' *Special Libraries*, 79 (4) Fall, 1988, pp. 271-276.

Williamson, Joan. One person libraries and information units: their education and training needs. *Library Management*, 9, (5), 1988.

Winston, Stephanie. *The Organized Executive*. New York: Warner, 1983.

Wood, Lawraine. *Marketing your information service*. Loughborough: Centre for Library and Information Management, 1985 (CLAIM Report No. 46).

Woolley, Marcus. 'The one-person library: professional development and professional managment.' *Library Management* 9, (1). Bradford, West Yorkshire: MCB Press, 1988.

Wright, Craig E., 'The corporate information challenge: streamlining external information,' *Records Management Quarterly* 25 (3) July, 1991. pp. 14-16.

Young, Arthur. *The Manager's Handbook*. New York: Crown, 1986.

'Your library's advocates: do you benefit from them?' Berner, Andrew, and St. Clair, Guy, eds. *The Best of OPL: Five Years of* The One–Person Library. Washington, D.C.: Special Libraries Association, 1990. pp. 48-49.

Index